Publishing Globally: Marketing Translation Rights Through Local Translators

INFAROM

Infarom Publishing
office@infarom.com
http://www.infarom.com

ISBN 978-973-1991-23-8

Publisher: **INFAROM**
Coordinator: **Doru Bărboianu**
Editor: **CarolAnn Johnson**

Copyright © INFAROM 2010

This work is subject to copyright. All rights are reserved, whether the whole work or part of the material is concerned, specifically the rights of translation, reprinting, reuse of diagrams, recitation, broadcasting, reproduction on microfilm or in any other way, and storage in data banks.
  Duplication of this publication or parts thereof is permitted only under the provisions of Copyright Laws, and permission for use must always be obtained from INFAROM.

Contents

Introduction	5
The Basic Description of the System	9
Publishers	21
Posting the Job	22
Selecting the Translator	29
Guarantees	31
Relationship with the Translator Before Starting the Activity	35
Closing a Deal	41
Translators	47
Applying for the Job	49
Relationship with the Original Publisher Before Starting the Activity	53
Translation	57
Marketing the Translation Rights	61
Database	63
Contacting Publishers	66
After Finding a Buying Publisher	75
Summary and Comments	77
Appendices	83

Introduction

Like every other trade nowadays, the book industry is experiencing the process of globalization. The worldwide political and economic changes last two decades not to mention development of the internet, have led to an ever-broadening scope of multidirectional international communication. And with this unlimited potential for communication comes an unprecedented opportunity for economic expansion.

The internet has become the primary means of communication as well as the major platform on which all participants in the book industry meet. Nowadays any author can submit his work to any publisher and contact any literary agent. Publishers can easily communicate with other publishers; agents can reach any publisher worldwide. The potential is limitless, all due to the power of the internet.

Even more significantly, however, due to this globalization and proliferation of book sales through the internet, large well-known publishers are no longer the only players who make the rules because the small and medium-sized presses now share the same means and web platforms to promote their titles. Of course, the greater financial resources of prominent publishing houses will still make a difference, keeping these large publishers at the top of the industry. However, with equal access to promotional resources, added to the more specialized service that a smaller publishing house can offer, these small presses stand poised to present significant competition in the book trade.

New POD (print-on-demand) technologies that print one book at a time depend entirely on electronic data transfer via the internet and require little to no human manipulation, making it possible – and highly desirable for economic reasons – to print books only as they are ordered. First ordering and then printing a book has significantly changed the way publishers do business.

Publishers with small budgets can increase the number of their published titles and gain great exposure thanks to the POD system. It should be noted that in the last few years, large publishers – many academic publishers being among them – have also adopted print-on-demand as part of their production.

Critics within the publishing industry are quick to point up the disadvantages of POD publishing, and these disadvantages are real; the most important of them is the questionable quality of the content – if anyone can publish anything, we can expect to find poor content on the market. Of course, these critics come mostly from large, well-known publishers who dislike competition. Still, the free market will itself resolve this issue: as in any other industry, poor quality products will eventually drive the producer out of business, and the publishing industry like every other, will be governed by the principle of supply and demand.

We have talked here about POD because, despite all its disadvantages, it is clearly the way to build a book market with equal access for every publisher. It is a natural consequence of globalization via internet, and most importantly, it is a fair system. Globalization of any domain will naturally generate such fair systems. Sellers of everything from furniture to fixtures have equal access to marketing worldwide. The publishing industry is no exception; in strong connection with this industry, the market of translations submits to the same globalization. Translations and linguistic projects from all over the world rely on web platforms to connect publishers and translators with each other. Thanks to the internet, virtually any set of languages within any field of expertise quickly finds translator services via web platforms.

For publishers, licensing the translation rights for some titles represents an important direction of development. Selling the translation rights in as many territories as possible is a marketing task generating a good stream of new revenues for already published titles.

How do publishers accomplish this task? The traditional way is to find a foreign rights agent or agency to represent the publisher abroad. Publishers can work with one agent or agency in each country or with agents or agencies covering several countries through their sub-agents. Another approach is for the publisher to market the translation rights directly to foreign publishers who specialize in the subject matter of the respective book. This latter method, however, consumes important internal resources of time and personnel and is usually not practiced by either large or small publishers, who prefer to work with agents instead.

Each foreign rights agent has his own manner of marketing titles in their respective territories. An agent most likely represents several publishers and numerous titles, and he must organize them by priority. But nobody – including the represented publishers – will know exactly what criteria the agent uses for ranking the represented titles and allocating a certain quantity of resources to each of them. And, of course, a publisher cannot control this allocation. A publisher can only submit its titles to the agent and wait for a foreign deal, no matter how long it takes for the deal to come through.

There are no rules for the process of licensing translation rights through agents or agencies, no recipe for success, and the outcome of such a marketing process is unpredictable. Just as there are no specific criteria by which to calculate prioritizing of titles, so also there are no proven criteria for selecting the right agent who, as noted before, markets the titles by a set of subjective and unpredictable rules. Therefore the movement of the titles in the foreign rights market is somehow chaotic under the traditional system. Of course, the well-known publishers have the biggest piece of cake of this market, because foreign publishers are usually inclined first to buy by the name of the original publisher, and second by title and content. Needless to say, despite the lack of predictability of agents' strategies, it can be safely assumed that the more well known the publisher, the higher priority its titles will take on an agent's list.

A system of marketing this particular commodity, similar to the POD publishing, would give equal exposure to all publishers who approach foreign buyers of translation licenses, just as POD publishing gives equal exposure of all publishers to the potential book buyer. After studying the global translation and foreign rights marketing phenomena in the last few years, our publishing house has developed and tested a system of marketing translation rights that will help to equalize opportunity for publishers in the international book trade.

This system – described in detail in the following chapters – aligns the interests and skills of all parties involved in the process of marketing translation rights and allocates the full amount of resources an agent can use for each particular represented title. The system is very natural, therefore simple, as it is based on supply and demand. It has key features that make it workable in any economic environment and provides advantages compared to the traditional approach to marketing translation rights. It aligns the right skills working for the right product to be promoted to the right market segment. And it introduces a new team member: the native translator, who has the opportunity to do translation in his field of expertise and get additional income beyond the payment for the translation itself.

The system addresses both publishers and translators. It is intended primarily as a development tool for small and medium publishers with small budgets, but large publishers can also use it to their advantage. Most importantly, anyone has access to this system. Its application requires minimal action – posting to a web platform – and minimal training. The information provided in this book is sufficient for both categories of users. Here readers will find a convenient guide through our system of publishing globally. A basic description of the system is followed by sections detailing each step toward completing the transaction.

It is our hope that readers will use and enjoy this guide!

The Basic Description of the System

The system we propose starts from the publishers' need to expand their sales in foreign countries, with high coverage and minimal costs. All publishers aim to sell translation rights for as many of their titles as possible in as many countries as possible.

Here is how the system typically works:

To market translation rights, a publisher works with a literary agent or agency who deals with foreign rights, passing to the agent the task of finding buyers in foreign countries, by using his resources, skills, and experience. With the price of the agent's commission, usually ten to twenty percent of the eventual deal, the publisher saves his own resources of time, money, and personnel, which can then be directed to the production of new titles instead of marketing the translation rights of the published ones. If the publisher does not have an agent to represent him, he must find one or more agents before attempting to license translation rights abroad. The agents can be located in the geographic zones to be covered or in the publisher's country of residence. Ordinarily, in this case, agents work with local sub-agents, who in turn receive commissions – usually five percent of the deals they close.

Finding agents to represent them is neither an easy nor a pleasant task for the publisher. It requires research and an extensive list of contacts. There are no proven objective criteria to select a trustworthy agent. An agent's portfolio (numbers of deals closed, local publishers he works with, publishers they represent, titles sold) might be an indication of the agent's potential, but these facts provide no guarantee that a publisher's particular titles will enjoy the same success.

Once a publisher has acquired an agent, he will provide the agent with all marketing data and materials necessary for presenting and promoting the submitted titles, along with reading copies of them.

When an agent finds a buyer in a country he covers, he will negotiate the deal on behalf of the represented publisher. The resulting contract will specify terms for translation and production, advance, royalties, and payment details. The agent will then undertake all formalities of signing the three-party contract. The agent will also monitor the post-contractual collaboration between the two publishers and mediate any disputes, including those arising over agreed payment. The local publisher who bought the translation rights then proceeds to work the translation in the time period agreed upon by both publishers.

While this would seem to be a straightforward and predictable arrangement, it holds certain drawbacks. In the following paragraphs, we consider the most important disadvantages, those relating to loss of time, reticence of the buying publisher, and quality of the translation.

A great deal of time is lost at every stage of the process. First, the publisher loses time searching for agents, if he is not already represented. As we saw above, the publisher must first locate, then evaluate a potential agent before any of the actual work of marketing begins. Second, having no control over when the agent effectively starts marketing the publisher's titles, the publisher should expect delays in this process. Third, more time is lost during the period in which the foreign publisher finishes the translation and puts the book in production, even though this particular time element may be stipulated in the contract.

A fourth disadvantage of the usual method of marketing foreign translations is the reticence of the foreign publisher. For a title of an unknown original publisher or a title that did not sell well in its original language, a foreign publisher may be hesitant about buying the translation rights. The fifth concern is that the foreign publisher might also hold reservations about working the translation, even if there seems to be good potential for that title – he might fear that the text is too difficult, with the risk of misinterpretation, or that it will consume too much of his resources.

The sixth drawback has to do with the quality of the translation. This is particularly true for specialized books. It is well known that an accurate translation can be done only by a translator whose fields of expertise include the topic of the book. The original publisher might not have a great deal of information about the local publisher who bought the translation rights (all he can see is the publisher's website), unless the company is well known or is a division of a multinational publisher. Knowing nothing about the size and resources of the foreign publisher, the original publisher might get a poor translation, if it was worked by a general translator rather than a specialized one. An inferior translation – even if the new title is published in a different country – still carries the name of the original publisher, and therefore, his reputation is adversely affected.

Some agencies have their own translator teams who work translations for the buying publishers. But the same issue could be raised regarding their translation, if the topic requires specialization.

The seventh disadvantage – related to the issue of lost production time – is that of the uncontrolled marketing of the agent: Dealing with a large number of titles coming from several publishers, the agent usually markets these titles in a block, grouped by categories, and gives priority to certain titles as selected by his personal criteria. The represented publisher cannot control the agent's management of titles and will never know whether his title receives the same amount of resources from the agent as other publishers' titles or even whether it has been marketed.

With one eye on these seven disadvantages and the other on the agent's activity, which is unpredictable and uncontrollable, we may say that the usual system of marketing translation rights is chaotic; success, especially for small publishers, is mostly a matter of luck. So how can we optimize the traditional system or even replace it with a better one?

Of course, one option is for the publisher to forego an agent's services and market the titles directly to foreign publishers. This, however, would require tremendous effort, consuming considerable resources for the publisher and affecting his entire operation. Consulting all directories, creating databases with foreign publishers' data, grouping them by specialty, contacting them via internet or mail, and presenting the marketed titles could easily occupy most of a small or medium-sized publisher's staff. Not only that, but many foreign publishers do not concur with such approach and prefer to search for titles themselves to be considered for translation, whether working with agents or not. A title offered via presentation letter or e-mail is unlikely to be considered by a foreign publisher because self-promotion automatically raises questions about the title's current success on the market.

Certainly this kind of marketing may work for some specialized titles offered to foreign publishers of the same field. However, this option is not one on which to rely entirely. At best, it can be combined with the typical way of working with agents.

Since publishers have become accustomed to using agents, let us see how we can improve the traditional system by finding hypothetical counterpoises to the seven previously described disadvantages.

The first three disadvantages mentioned previously concern the time factor.

- Question: How can the publisher save time in searching for agents?
Answer: By having the agents come to him, then selecting from them.
- Question: How can the publisher control the marketing practices of his agent, and the priority that agent gives to the

publisher's title? (This question also addresses the seventh issue – that of the marketing time frame.)

Answer: By introducing a motive for the agent to rush the marketing of that title.

Another answer: By having an agent who markets only that title or at most just a few titles.

- How can the represented publisher and the agent rush the buying publisher to publish the translation?

Answer: By providing the finished translation already worked by a translator procured by the original publisher or his agent.

The next issues concern the reticence of a foreign publisher to accept a particular title or an original publisher who is not well known.

- Question: How can the agent lessen the foreign publisher's reticence toward a questionable title or publisher?

Answer: We could not find a hypothetical solution to completely resolve this issue – and perhaps it does not exist – but the solution to the third disadvantage above, presenting the buying publisher a finished translation, gives the title an additional chance: having the translation (or a substantial translated sample) in front of the foreign publisher, he can go through its content and evaluate it quickly, which is usually much more difficult or even impossible when the content is in the original language. Even for languages with wide circulation, that step requires additional time and internal resources.

- Question: How can the agent reduce the reticence of the foreign publisher about working the translation?

Answer: The same answer as above applies here: By providing the translation itself, already completed.

- Question: How can the original publisher influence the execution of a correct translation by a competent translator?

Answer: Again, these concerns may be resolved by providing the buying publisher with the translation itself, in this case, done by a translator who is native in that foreign language and specializes in the topic of that particular book.

All of the above hypothetical solutions expressed in these answers may enhance the traditional method of marketing foreign translations if these solutions can be combined in a real, non-contradictory, functional system.
Well, such a system is possible.

What hypothetical participants does the publisher need in order to make that system work? Actually, only two: A translator both native in the target language and specialized in the topic of the marketed title, and a local agent who will market only that title at that time. The former is easy to find, as the translation market is a large one and usually the supply exceeds the demand for such services. However, the latter, traditional foreign-rights agents, are quite difficult if not impossible to find. What if the native translator could also function as the publisher's agent? In order to represent the publisher and the title translated, the translator should reside in the country of his native language. This requirement can be stipulated in the posted job description.

A local translator working also as the original publisher's agent in his country – hereafter termed "translator-agent" – offers a perfect solution to the various problems described above. The publisher can find such a translator-agent by posting this job on internet platforms because there are also good motivations for a translator for such a job. For example:
- The translator-agent will receive income from two sources rather than one. First, there is payment for the translation itself (paid by the foreign publisher), and second, the agent's commission for a translation rights sale (paid by the hiring publisher), which consists of both a commission from the advance and that from future royalties.

- The translator-agent will enrich his portfolio. A translated book carries greater weight than other works, and his name will also appear on the copyright page of the new book.
- The translator-agent will be working in his precise field of expertise. The concerns over awkward or incorrect interpretations will therefore be greatly reduced.
- Such transactions will open doors to further opportunities for collaboration with both publishers.

Of course there is always the risk that the translator may not find a buyer for the translated title after he has completed the work of translation. And so the system needs just one more element to make it completely functional: some arrangement or financial guarantee from the hiring publisher to cover – entirely or partially – the risk assumed by the translator-agent of not selling the translation rights. Without such a guarantee, the publisher risks finding no applicants for the job, finding them only after a lengthy search, or attracting too few applicants to make an optimal selection.

Such guarantees can take the form of a partial payment of the translation work – for example, fifty percent of the agreed-upon fee, the balance being paid after the sale, from the foreign publisher's portion. Alternatively, the full amount – or nothing at all – can be paid in advance. Another option is for the translator-agent to hold co-author status with royalties for an edition to be published in that foreign language by the original publisher himself, should both the translator-agent and the original publisher fail to find a buyer for those rights. Each publisher can set up his own guarantee package for his translator-agent. We shall talk in detail about these compensatory arrangements in the section dedicated to the guarantees.

So in summary, the original publisher creates his own agent profile: a translator native in the target language, living in that specific country, who will market only this publisher's titles in that territory. Besides posting the job and selecting the individual, the original publisher must train the new agent on how to do an agent's job and provide him with all needed materials. We shall discuss this training in detail in a later section.

Now let us see how the translator-agent system works chronologically. We refer to the three trading partners as follows:

Translator-agent – the translator acting as a foreign-rights agent

Selling publisher – the publisher who published the title in the original language and wishes to market its translations rights abroad

Buying publisher – the foreign publisher who buys the translation rights from the selling publisher.

- The selling publisher posts the translator-agent job in the media.
- Independent translators apply for this job.
- The selling publisher selects from among the applicants one person with whom he signs a contract of translation and representation. This contract must include:
  - terms and deadlines for translation and marketing
  - monetary compensation for the carried services
  - guarantees against the risks described above
- The translator-agent does the translation and delivers it to the selling publisher.
- The selling publisher trains the translator-agent for the marketing activity, providing him with all needed materials (copies of the original title, sale statistics, eventual reviews, presentation letters, etc.). The selling publisher also provides the translator-agent with a letter of introduction verifying that he is the publisher's representative and is acting in his behalf.
- The translator-agent offers and promotes the title to publishers from his country through direct contacts.
- If the translator-agent fails to make a sale, the selling publisher takes over the marketing activity on his own, continuing independently or through traditional foreign-rights agents. If the

traditional system also fails to find a buyer, the selling publisher could publish the foreign edition under his imprint and put it on global channels such as Ingram distribution, giving the translator-agent the agreed guarantees (partial or full payment of translation work or royalties on the new edition).

• If the translator-agent makes the sale, he will put both publishers in direct contact with each other, and this relationship will become the standard one in the licensing translation rights process, starting with the signing of the contract. The translator-agent will be paid for the translation work by the selling publisher, who was in turn paid by the buying publisher. Then he will receive commissions each time they are paid from the royalties that the selling publisher receives from the buying publisher.

Now let us enumerate the advantages of the translator-agent system, from each partner's point of view:

<u>Advantages for the selling publisher:</u>
• He can expect to get the best possible translation both through selection of the translators and the fact that they share a joint financial interest;
• The selling publisher is able to offer the completed translation to foreign publishers;
• The native translator is familiar with his respective country, language, and local trade behaviors and habits, and thus is able to provide the most effective approach to local publishers;
• The selling publisher avoids loss of a considerable amount of time by having the entire translation and marketing process under his own control;
• The selling publisher can anticipate low costs – possibly no cost – for the campaigns, a significant benefit for small presses;

- The selling publisher enjoys the possibility of also making a profit from the translation payment (which is paid by the buying publisher);
- The new title will be published relatively quickly, having the translation already done before approaching the buying publisher.

<u>Advantages for the translator</u>
- The translator has the benefit of working on a translation with which he is comfortable, for which he applied, in his field of expertise;
- There is the opportunity for additional (regular) income besides the translation payment;
- The translator will enrich his portfolio with a book;
- The translator benefits from the possibility of having a further permanent collaboration with both publishers after closing a deal.

<u>Advantages for the buying publisher</u>
- The buying publisher will not have to use his resources for translation; he has a high-quality, print-ready translation, which means quicker publishing.
- The agent with whom the publisher deals is native to his customs and language.

There is one single disadvantage of the translator-agent system: The translator lacks the experience and skills of a traditional foreign rights agent. But this disadvantage is offset by the following conditions: first, the translator-agent is focused on a single title once, knowing its entire content (as he has translated it). The content presentation could compensate for other marketing tips the translator might not be familiar with. Second, the selling publisher will provide the translator-agent with basic training regarding an agent's responsibilities.

Even potentially inadequate marketing will still be counterbalanced by presenting the completed translation, which is the key element of the proposed system. Foreign publishers usually ask those who market their translation rights about available resources to work the translation. Having the content done beforehand always indicates minimal outlay of resources and time for the foreign publishers and is thus an important criterion for them when acquiring licenses.

The next diagram presents the format of the translator-agent system with the functional relationship between involved partners.

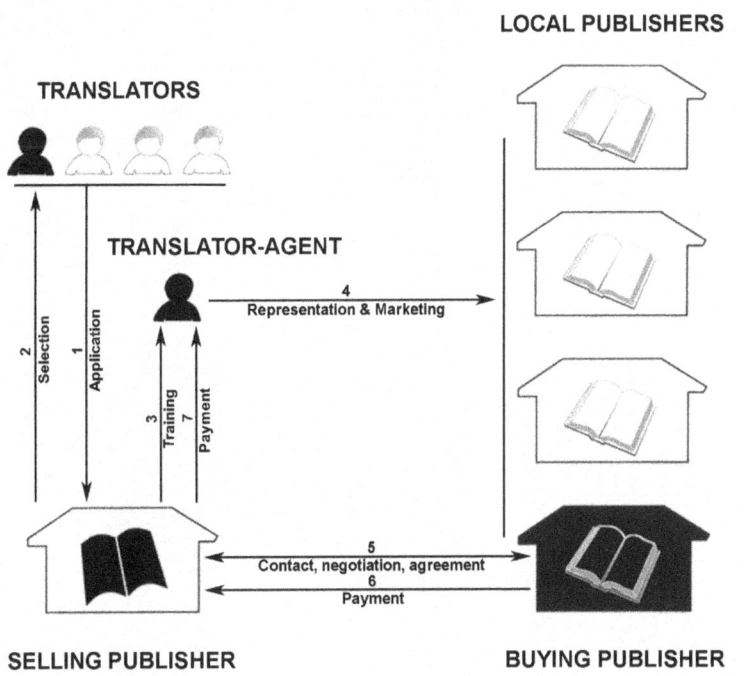

We have thus far presented a brief description of our proposed publishing system. The next two chapters are addressed to publishers and translator-agents, respectively. These chapters provide a thorough explanation of all stages of the process as related to each party.

Publishers

Selling translation rights to a book is an increasingly essential part of a publisher's management in today's global market. Not only does the translated title provide new sources of revenue for the publisher, author, and others involved in this endeavor, but every translated title that a publisher manages promotes that publisher's name abroad. Additionally, one title translated and published in several countries provides an excellent source of advertising for that publisher's forthcoming titles.

Several conditions must be considered in selecting titles to be promoted abroad. First of all, the publisher must be aware of the compatibility of selected titles with the market to which it is directed. Even if the book in question sold well in its country of origin, it will not necessarily attract the attention or interest of publishers abroad. People of different cultures share vastly different backgrounds and interests, so a book that is successful in its country of origin might not have the same appeal outside that country. For example, specific local history such as the conversion of a landmark building will likely be of interest only to persons in that particular country or with connections to that community.

Even though the book may cover a subject directed to a wider audience, there are other factors to consider. For one thing, foreign publishers usually seek titles whose content is not yet available in their language – a novel of fiction, perhaps, or for an esoteric readership, a political treatise. Another issue concerns time-sensitive material; for instance, a book covering an international event of the current year will take months to translate and publish abroad, and thus will lose appeal to readers interested in that event. Still another factor to be considered is the page count of the translation. As an example, a novel originally written in U.S. English can double its volume when translated into Dutch; conversely, an Asian translation of the same work will run roughly half the number of pages of its English counterpart. Foreign rights agents typically know the local markets as well as the needs and interests of the foreign buying publishers, and therefore, they will select from the titles offered by the selling publisher those they believe have good sales potential. In fact, that is their job!

In our proposed system, a publisher will not submit selected titles *in block* to the foreign rights agent, but will instead offer each title as a separate job posting for which interested translator-agents may apply. This strategy requires that publishers select titles carefully, according to the previously mentioned criteria, to avoid wasting resources on titles that have little or no sales potential for foreign buying publishers. The selling publisher controls all of the processes of this system, and for the most part, all of the later activity of the translator-agent.

The first step is to post the specific job where it will reach potential applicants.

Posting the Job

The first requisite in this system is that each job posted in the media shall represent only one title. This approach helps to ensure that applicants have both interest and expertise in working with that particular title or specialty. Posting on the Internet should provide enough exposure for the job; this venue has rapidly become the first – often the only – place applicants look for job listings. The following types of web platforms are likely to attract a sufficiency of qualified applicants:

- Translation marketplaces such as ProZ.com where the job advertisement is posted as a project for which translators submit a price quote.
- General job websites: on this type of platform, it is important to post in the correct category, namely "translations," and the correct industry, namely "publishing"; as a job listing of this type is uncommon, it may be necessary to adjust the posting somewhat in order to accommodate the format and fields of the web forms of that particular website.
- Translators' forums: these platforms assume a friendlier tone in a message posted as a new thread describing the job. One risk in posting on a forum is that if the forum does not provide a "jobs" topic, the forum administrator might ban the posting as inappropriate, spam, or the like. Such a situation might be avoided by contacting the administrator directly as to its acceptability before attempting to post the job.
- Websites dedicated to the translator-agent system: on such websites, the posting uses web forms with fields for the specific elements of a particular job – for example, job title, pair of languages involved, guarantees, agent's commission, requirements for the translator, and so on. A web form such as this eliminates the need for a job description *per se*, as the system is described within that website's content.

Of course it goes without saying that your own website will include a page dedicated to this job with functionality for applying directly from the website. Additionally, postings on the third-party sites listed above should, where allowed, include a link to your website.
Providing such a link is recommended especially when posting on forums, in order to shorten the content of the posted message.
The job advertisement itself should state that the job requires the translator-agent system, with details upon request or a link directing the applicant to such details. The ad may or may not include the compensation offered for the translation (this

amount will most likely be negotiated between yourself and the selected translator); if the amount is mentioned in the ad, it should also specify who actually pays for the translation – for example, the buying publisher pays one hundred percent or you and the buying publisher each pay fifty percent.

The ad should also include other financial details such as the guarantees and commissions offered. Guarantees might take the form of a share of the translation payment (our recommendation is fifty percent) or royalties on future editions under the selling publisher's imprint, or both. If you offer no guarantees, naturally you should avoid mentioning this in the ad. Agent commissions generally represent a percentage of the gross deal (we recommend five to eight percent).

Whether a web form is provided or not, the ad must supply data about the job itself: book title, content description, literary genre, category/subcategory of the topic, and the number of pages. Optionally, the ad may mention that a sample of the text is available upon request.

Following the job description are requirements for the translator. The fundamental requirements are for the translator to be native in the target language and a resident in the country in which the selling publisher intends to sell translation rights to the title in question. You may also specify other requirements such as age and experience level, a particular professional background (essential for specialized books), certain computer skills, and so forth.

Of course the ad must indicate the pair of languages specific to this job (from [original language of the title] to [language of the territory in which the translation is to be sold]). It is possible to include several pairs of languages if the platform on which the posting appears allows such. Some platforms allow only one pair of languages for each posted project. Needless to say, a different translator-agent is required for each language pair.

At the end of the ad, the applicant should find instructions for submitting his application. These instructions include the type of application (resume, letter of intent, e-mail, web form) as well as the physical address if the web platform does not offer its own functionality for applications.

Finally, in addition to providing all of the above information, the posting should give the key elements of a job of this type: the opportunity for two sources of income for the translator and the dual nature of the applicant's responsibilities, namely translating and then marketing the title. In summary, the ad should present complete information, disclosing all risk involved so as not to mislead by omission of pertinent details.

Following are some examples of ads, one for each category of website on which the job might be posted.

1. For a translation marketplace (ProZ.com format of job posting used)

Job title: Translators-agents required for history book
Job type: Translation/editing/proofing job
  Services required: Translation, Checking/editing

Languages: English to Norwegian, English to Swedish

Job description:
[*Name of publisher*] is looking for native translators to translate our book titled *Unknown Medieval Legends of the Northern Europe*. We are looking for translators to work in a translator-agent system. This means you work the translation and then offer the translation rights to the local publishers in your country of residence. You will be paid for the translation work (as a negotiable fee) 50% by us as a guarantee, and 50% by the buying publisher plus 8% commission on future transactions (from advance and regular royalties). More details about this system can be found at [*URL of a webpage holding details about the translator-agent system*]. One translator per language will

be selected. More details about the job upon request. Applicants should send a résumé to [*publishername@host.com*]; the subject field should indicate the book title and applicant's language.

The book is a compilation of very old texts regarding historical and mystical legends that circulated by oral means in 16th and 17th centuries in the Northern countries of Europe, which were not mentioned in the classical history books.

Source format: Microsoft Word

Delivery format: Microsoft Word

Budget and payment details:
Further payment details: translation work plus commissions of 8% of the translation rights transaction
Payment method: Online via PayPal or wire transfer
Payment 3 days after date of delivery.
Volume: 200 pages

Service provider targeting:
Preferred expertise: Art/Literary, Social Science
Preferred specific fields: History, Folklore
Subject field: History
Preferred software: Microsoft Word

Additional requirements:
Candidates should be native in the target language and residents of that country.
Candidates must have relevant experience in book translation and between the ages of 30 and 60.
Education degree or a personal interest in ancient European history is a plus.
Background in working with local publishers is also a plus.

2. For job websites

Job title: Translators-agents required; translation and promotion of cookbook
Available positions: 1
Offer type: project-based
Career level: Senior level
Job domains: Media/Culture/Publications
Countries: Bulgaria
Cities: any

Net salary offered: not mentioned/negotiable

Job description:
US-based publisher is looking for a native translator to translate our book titled "100 Quick Recipes: How to Make Royal Meals in Minutes" and promote it to local publishers. We are looking for a translator to work in a translator-agent system, which consists of translation, contacting the local publishers, and promoting the book to them. You will be paid for the translation work (a negotiable fee) by the publisher who buys the translation rights and also 8% commission of the transaction (from advance and regular royalties). Guarantees offered in royalties on a future edition published by us. More details about this system can be found at [*URL of a webpage holding details about the translator-agent system*].
Translator-agent may work at home. Basic training is provided from distance. The book has 250 pages (about 50,000 words) .

Requirements:
Candidates should be native in Bulgarian and reside in this country. Candidates must have relevant experience in book translation and between the ages of 30 and 60.
Candidates should have a good command of Microsoft Word and Excel, and good internet-browsing skills.
Background in working with local publishers is a plus.

Bonuses, benefits:
After completing this project, you have the opportunity to remain a permanent collaborator with us and the local publisher acquiring the translation rights.

Company's data:
Company's name: *Name of publisher*
Field of activity: Publishing
Description: Publishing house specializing in "how-to" books
Résumé: In English

3. For translators' forums

In one of these sub-forums: Jobs, Miscellaneous, Advertising, etc.

Subject of the new thread: translators working as literary agents needed / two types of revenue for a translation work / publisher seeks translators-agents for novel /

Message:
Hi everyone,
I represent [*Name of publisher*], who is seeking native translators in German and Japanese for a translation of our novel *The Ring of the Emperor*. This job submits to the newest system in publishing translations, which combines the translation with local marketing of the translation rights and offers the translator two types of revenue: the translation work payment and commissions on the transaction of licensing the foreign rights. More details about this system at [*URL of a webpage holding details about the translator-agent system*].
We offer training, support, financial guarantees, and 7% royalties on the new language edition. The translation fees are negotiable.
The requirements for the translator-agent are: native in the target language, resident of that country and education with philological background.
We remain at your disposal for any questions on this forum or for sample text requests.

Selecting the Translator

When you have received enough applications, or when the posted deadline for submitting applications has passed, the selection process begins. One translator-agent will be chosen, or many, if the job posting required translation in several languages. The selection criteria must necessarily include the following (in our recommended order of importance):

1) The translator should be native in the target language and a resident of that country. As discussed earlier, the agent's familiarity with the customs and culture of a region plays an important role in his success with local publishers, and residency helps to assure familiarity.

2) The translator should possess a strong background and/or education in philology.

3) The translator should be experienced in doing translations of the type of work intended (fiction, instructional materials, specialized topics, and so forth).

4) The translator should have collaborated in the past with publishers from his country of residence, or if he does not have this experience, the applicant should have at least some public relations or sales background.

5) The translator should have a strong degree of expertise in the field of the book's specialization.

6) The translator should present an adequate portfolio.

7) The translator should fall within the age range specified in the ad.

The above criteria will obviously be ascertained by reading the submitted résumés. Of course, some of these criteria – for example, the age requirement – can be applied only if enough applications are received to allow such selection. The manner in which the criteria are aggregated and the weight each of them holds in the selection of an applicant are subjective and depend at least partly on the preferences of each individual publisher.

One last point to consider – and this factor falls outside the selection criteria and key points of the résumé: it is important to select a person who loves his work and who puts greater value on seeing his name on a well translated book than on the maximum dollar amount he could receive. Such an intangible attribute can be identified only from an applicant's letter of intent; of course, such a claim amounts to self-representation and is thus not verifiable.

The selection of the right translator-agent is critical to making this system work, because that individual is the person who will effectively produce and sell your product. However, as with any selection of applicants, finding the right person depends upon a measure of luck as well as discretion. The right résumé does not necessarily guarantee the right person. Only the performance of the selected individual can confirm the choice.

What if the "wrong" person were selected? What would that mean in this situation? It is unlikely that a translator's credentials would be falsified, since intentional deception would quickly become apparent; some translators' marketplaces offer credentials verification, and some provide reviews of previously worked translation projects. So in fact, the "wrong" person may be one who holds the necessary qualifications, but due to various other factors, simply delays the translation and/or marketing, or perhaps takes an ineffective marketing approach toward local publishers.

These risks can be minimized in two ways: first, by careful and thorough training of the selected translator-agent, and second, by contractual clauses covering deadlines and results. We shall discuss these types of clauses in a later section which details the contract between the hiring publisher and the translator-agent.

Guarantees

The newly selected translator-agent will of course require some assurance, before beginning the project, against the risks inherent in the translator-agent arrangement:
- First, there is the risk of failure to find a buyer for the translation rights. Should this occur, there will be no party responsible for paying the translator for his work.
- Second, the translator risks the potential loss of other standard translation jobs during the time allocated to this project.

To compensate for such risks, you should offer certain guarantees for the translator before starting the collaboration.

Each publisher may establish his own formula for creating a guarantee package, which will consist of two types of compensation:

1) **A percentage of the payment for the translation work.**
You will recover this amount from the buying publisher who pays for the entire translation job. The translator-agent will receive this guarantee if he does the translation, but fails to sell its rights. If he does sell the rights, you will pay the full amount for the translation work – either after you receive payment from the buying publisher, or possibly prior to this if you have reason to be confident that the deal will go through with no complications.

Our recommendation is for the selling publisher to offer fifty percent of the contracted price for the translation as security. The reason for this proposed amount is that the fifty-fifty variant always induces a perception of fairness – the translator-agent and the selling publisher assume equal amounts of financial risk. If you choose a higher guaranteed amount – say seventy to eighty percent – it is more advantageous for you to pay the translator-agent for the entire translation, one hundred percent, because then if the translator-agent sells the rights, you will receive your share from the buying publisher, and if not, there will be no need for additional compensation in royalties for the translator (see the next section).

2) **Royalties on a future edition in that foreign language.**
If both the translator-agent and you yourself fail to sell the translation rights through either our system or conventional methods, you may choose to publish the translated edition yourself. When the translator-agent passes the deadline specified in the contract for finding a buyer, you may take this task upon yourself using the traditional approaches for marketing translation rights. If you also fail to find a buyer, there is still the choice to publish that foreign edition under your own imprint and place it on the global market. In this case, you can offer the translator-agent a co-author status (which actually he is, as translator), and royalties on this eventual edition. We recommend five percent as guaranteed royalties for the translator-agent. This recommendation takes into account your royalties and the large discounts offered in the global distribution network, since you will not sell the book directly in the territory of that foreign language.

These two types of guarantees can be offered in any arrangement. For example, you can offer only payment for the translation or only royalties once the translation is published, or both types of compensation in various combinations. You can also, in fact, offer none of them. However, if you should choose this option, the translator-agent will have no guarantee of payment after finishing the job. Therefore, this option is not recommended, as your applicant selection base will diminish significantly.

Here are some examples of guarantee packages in case of the translator-agent's failure to acquire a buying publisher for the translated edition:

1) – payment of 30% of the translation work and
   – royalties of 3% on the eventual foreign edition.

2) – no payment for the translation work and
   – royalties of 7% on the eventual foreign edition.

3) – payment of 50% of the translation work and
   – royalties of 3% on the eventual foreign edition.

4) – payment of 50% of the translation work and
   – no royalties on the eventual foreign edition.

The guarantees come into effect according to the following schedule:
- the payment for translation work is made after the translator-agent delivers the translation and before he starts the marketing activity;
- the royalties begin to be paid after the deadline for the translator-agent's activity and after the new edition has been produced and put in distribution.

All the offered guarantees and the above time frames should be spelled out in the contract you sign with the translator-agent. You have the option to negotiate the guarantees with the translator-agent prior to signing the contract instead of establishing them beforehand and describing them in the job ads. If you prefer to proceed in this direction, the job ad must state that guarantees are negotiable. We strongly recommend this negotiation, as it may increase the number of applicants and it creates the impression of flexibility on your part.

One further note seems in order regarding production of a foreign edition: you should be aware that your own editions will enjoy fewer sales than they would through a foreign publisher. The publisher in the intended area will distribute that title locally to physical retailers, having far greater coverage of that territory than may be obtained through other eventual international distributors.

The most cost-effective option is for you to produce the book in a POD system and place it in global distribution, through a distributor such as Ingram's. The title will then be listed by the largest web retailers such as Amazon, Barnes&Noble, and book marketplaces like Alibris, AbeBooks, and others, and will of course reach some foreign customers through these web channels. However, a local publisher will reach more customers in his native territory than you could reach through these online channels.

Of course, after publishing your own foreign edition, you can at any time sell the translation rights to a foreign publisher, if you continue the marketing through standard methods. In this case, you will withdraw the current title from distribution under your own name and cede it to the buying publisher.

Relationship with the Translator Before Starting the Activity

Once you have selected the candidate who will work with you in the translator-agent system for a specific territory and language, the next step will be a round of discussions to clarify expectations for the job and to settle all terms of the collaboration. These discussions may simply take the form of a continuation of the question-and-answer sessions that took place during the application phase. The entire communication will be conducted via e-mail or telephone, in your language, which, it is assumed, both parties know well.

The goal of the first series of discussions is to familiarize the translator with the basics of the translator-agent system and to answer any questions he may have about how the system works. Answering the translator's questions is the most important part of this dialogue.

During this part of the discourse, you should direct the translator to materials published on the internet as well as any available printed manuals that present this system. It would be most helpful to offer this book to study if the candidate does not already own it. This first round of discussions is actually the first stage of training that you must conduct for the translator. During the second set of conversations, you and the translator will negotiate the financial terms of the collaboration (if you have chosen to allow this).

When negotiating terms of the contract, four points must be considered: the translator's fee for translation work (usually stated per 300-word page or per word of the source document), the agent's commission for a sale, the guarantees, and the deadlines – first for delivery of the translation, and second for completing the sale to a buying publisher.

When settling on the translation fee, it is not wise to push too much, since the buying publisher will ultimately pay this fee.

Even so, you will want to parley a lower fee in order to increase the profit when selling for a higher price to the buying publisher.

One point in persuading the translator to accept a lower fee than usual is the compensation from the second income – namely, the agent commissions – that the translator-agent will receive. You might also choose another approach: you can accept the fee that the translator asks and thus save the negotiating points for the remaining elements of the financial agreement. Needless to say, this approach is not recommended if you pay the full translation fee as a guarantee. In this case, obtaining the lowest possible translation fee is most profitable.

The second point of consideration in financial negotiations is that of the agent commission. We recommend an amount between five and eight percent of the final deal, but the amount can go as high as ten percent, depending on the rest of the financial package agreed upon. This recommendation is based upon the following limitations: the commission should be less than a traditional literary agent or agency charges (usually ten to fifteen percent) but higher than the lowest commissions offered in any trade (usually somewhere between two and five percent.) The first limitation is justified by the fact that the translator-agent lacks the resources, professional connections, and power of a traditional agent; the translator-agent also does less work.

Negotiation of the third point, guarantees, should take into account the amount agreed upon for the first two factors, translation fee and commissions. Your choice to pay a portion of the translation work in advance is contingent upon your own budget. Then, the royalties on a forthcoming foreign edition should be subtracted from the original author's royalties on this foreign edition. The original author and the translator will then split the royalties; each publisher has his own formula for splitting royalties. For our purposes here, we recommend a fifty-fifty split. For example, if the author receives eight percent royalties on the original edition, the foreign edition published by the same publisher should retain this same amount, but it will be split between the two co-authors – the original author and the translator, each receiving four percent.

If the foreign edition is published by a local publisher abroad, the standard royalties paid by the foreign publisher to the original publisher are five to ten percent of the new list price. In the case at hand, the translator-agent will receive commissions on these royalties beyond the translation work. As an example, if you agree on an eight-percent agent commission and you receive seven percent royalties on these commissions from the foreign publisher, then the translator-agent will receive eight percent of seven percent or 0.56 percent of the new list price for each book sold.

The final point in contract negotiations is the deadlines – one for translation and the other for finding a buyer. We recommend six months for the latter. As for the translation delivery, try to accept the translator's date.

If you and the candidate are unable to reach an agreement on the terms of your collaboration, you may either accept or reject the translator's terms, depending on whether there are other qualified applicants from which to choose. If other applicants are available, you may turn down the present candidate and move to the next individual on the list.

If the contract negotiations do, however, end in agreement, the next step is the signing of the contract for translation and representation. This contract should contain the following elements:

- Description of the activity expected of the translator-agent as well as the obligations of both parties required to make such activity workable
- Execution deadlines
- Payments and their time frames
- Translation warranty
- Detailed guarantees offered by the publisher
- Copyright terms

A model of the contract may be found in the *Appendices* section of this book.

The contract should be sent to the translator in electronic form or by postal mail (at least two copies if sent via post); the translator should then sign and return all copies by postal mail to you; you will then in turn remit one countersigned copy to the translator. After the contract is signed by both parties, the collaboration has begun.

The next form you must send to the translator-agent is a document verifying that the bearer (agent) is your representative and acts on your behalf for marketing the translation rights of your titles in the respective territory. Such a document may be required by local publishers as – or in addition to – identification. The document can be an ID card or simply a letter of introduction. Whichever form is used, the document should include a photograph of the individual and your stamp as proof of validity. A model of this document also can be found in the *Appendices* section of this book.

After agreeing on all financial terms and deadlines, and subsequently signing the contract and issuing the necessary forms, the next round of communication continues the training process.

Initially, you must inform the translator-agent of the content he will translate – in other words, the subject, genre, and style of the work – and what is expected from the translation. The translator should be made aware of any specific language difficulties he may encounter such as esoteric or idiomatic terminology, semantics and shades of meaning, or even the necessity of changing some wording to conform not only to the foreign language of the translation, but also to differences in culture and place. And of course there are always those words that are simply "untranslatable." Generally speaking you should teach the translator what you know about the content that the translator does not know. During the actual translation work, you should offer continuous support to the translator, answering any questions he might have about the text. It is important to maintain regular communication with the translator in order to observe the progress of the work and to be aware of any issues he may encounter. You may suggest that the translator work directly on the editable source document, which you have already provided. By working in this mode, the translator will save time and preserve the design of the page. We refer here especially to insertions such as images, graphs, charts, schematics, tables, and the like. By preserving the design through the editing process, the document will be almost print-ready when the translation is done. You will only have to make some final adjustments and repaginate the book.

One more phase of training remains: that of the agent activity. This portion of training covers two primary activities, establishing a database and making direct contact with publishers.

You must teach the translator, if he does not already know, how to set up a database of local publishers. The translator needs to understand where to find the required data, how to organize it, and how to use this data when contacting publishers.

You will also most likely need to instruct the translator-agent in the standard procedures of the industry: the first contact (usually via e-mail or postal letter), scheduling appointments, steps in approaching the publisher, presentation of the marketed title, and tips for attracting the interest of the publisher. You will also provide all materials needed to accomplish the task. These materials include models of a presentation letter, title description, marketing data (for example, projected sales statistics of the original title, reviews, published references, and so forth), and your full contact information. Naturally, it is not enough to simply present these data; the buying publisher will need to be convinced that the title being marketed represents good sales potential for him. And therefore, you must also make the translator-agent aware of how the title he is marketing is different from similar offerings in the same category and why a foreign edition holds promise for this particular territory. All of these concerns will addressed much more fully in the section directed to translators.

After finishing the translation, completing the training regarding agent activity, and establishing the contact database, the translator-agent may begin marketing the translation rights to local publishers. Along with the ID verification document and the marketing materials mentioned earlier, you must provide the translator-agent with a sample of his translation in its final form. This sample could be a PDF document. We recommend using an incomplete sample (perhaps eighty to ninety percent of the full content, with some whole sections missing) in order to avoid copyright theft. Unfortunately, not all of the publishers contacted by the translator-agent will be scrupulous and above-board, and thus it is safer to protect against such theft.

Finally, we reiterate the necessity to maintain continuous contact with the translator-agent, answering all of his questions and reinforcing his training at every stage of the marketing process.

Closing a Deal

When the translator-agent finds a local publisher interested in purchasing the translation rights to a title, you will then take over the entire interaction and communication with the potential buyer from that point forward. From here on, the relationship between you and the buying publisher follows the standard procedure for licensing translation rights, the main parts of which are the pre-deal communication and negotiation of the deal itself.

Before beginning any negotiations, it is highly recommended that you investigate the foreign publisher and learn as much as possible about him, including his reputation in the business, the number of titles he has published each year, and a list of other publishers from whom he has previously acquired translation rights. The next step, then, is to contact those publishers for references about him.

The translator-agent should have provided the foreign publisher with all materials necessary for him to consider the marketed title, including a copy of the original book and a sample portion of the translated edition. Therefore, prior to contract negotiations, the two parties must decide upon the length of the review period. You agree during this period not to market that title where that language is predominant. However, during the agreed-upon review period, negotiations continue between you and the buying publisher regarding the translation itself, the fee for translating, and of course the benefits to the foreign publisher of having a completed translation done by a qualified individual and ready for printing. This last point is the additional component to the standard procedure of licensing translation rights, and is potentially the most significant selling point offered by the selling publisher. As such, it should be discussed and reiterated from the beginning and throughout the negotiations.

Assuming that the foreign publisher has decided to purchase this title, the next step is to negotiate the terms of the deal. Key terms of this negotiation will include the territory covered by the contract, the royalty advance and royalty terms, the term of the contract, the selling price of the foreign edition, quantity of the first printing, and the fee for the translation. The specific stipulations and conditions will vary from one deal to another and from one foreign language to another.

Contract negotiations should begin by establishing the specific language and territory covered by the contract. This decision must be made before continuing into discussions of the royalty advance and rate.

To illustrate the nature and importance of this point, consider Spanish, a language spoken not only in Spain, but also in Latin America. If you license Spanish rights but fail to specify a territory in the contract, the foreign (buying) publisher could also sell the Spanish edition in Bolivia or Costa Rica, areas in which you might otherwise find a local publisher, thereby benefiting sales in that country.

Besides the fact that Spanish is spoken in numerous countries, there are linguistic distinctions within a country or even within a locale. For instance, Castilian, Galician, and Basque are all dialects of Spanish found in Spain. Castilian is also spoken in Mexico and Argentina, so a Castilian edition might be more suitable, and thus more profitable, in those countries.

Another illustrative example is that of China, whose language uses either "traditional written characters" (primarily in Hong Kong and Taiwan) or "simplified characters" (used in Mainland China as well as other Asian countries such as Singapore and Malaysia). When negotiating translation rights for Chinese language editions, it is important to specify not only the particular countries to be covered, but also the Chine character system to be included in the language grant.

For these kinds of situations, it is obvious that agreement between both parties on language and territorial rights is crucial since the specifics of these grants could strongly impact the royalty advance and royalty income that you receive.

The next point for consideration is the royalty rate and advance. The royalty rate for the list price of a book varies from country to country and usually falls between five and ten percent for the first printing. The rate also depends upon the subject of the book. Usually, the buying publisher offers an amount for the royalty rate and royalty advance. The selling publisher should first negotiate the royalty rate; the royalty advance will be determined by the rate.[1]

A standard estimation may be found using the following algorithm:

1) Estimate the unit sales potential of the proposed title;
2) Determine a minimum retail selling price for the book in that territory (this may be obtained from the buying publisher);
3) Compute an estimate of the royalty the selling publisher will receive when the first printing is sold out;
4) To obtain the royalty advance amount, divide the amount obtained in Step 3 by two.

Here is an example applying this formula:
Retail price is $12.
First printing is 3,000 copies, retailing for $36,000.
Royalty rate on the first printing is 8%.
Royalty earned on the first printing is $36,000 × 8% = $2880.
Therefore, the royalty advance is $2880 ÷ 2 = $1440.

The next item for negotiation is the price that the foreign publisher will pay you for the translation. (This figure is, of course, in addition to the future royalties.) You should not be too adamant on this point. Depending on how much interest the

---

Reference for this section:
[1] Lloyd L. Rich [2000, 2001]: *Licensing Translation Rights*, article, Publishing Law Center

foreign publisher has in that title, and how difficult the translation is, you may request a higher price; however, even though you may be tempted to ask a price much higher than he will actually pay to the translator, such an approach may pose an obstacle for the eventual deal. The general recommendation is to ask a fair price, not a great deal higher than the translator's actual fee, bearing in mind that this potential buyer might be the only one in that territory interested in this particular title.

Even though the royalty rate and advance are negotiated first, the price of the translation is the first payment to be made by the buying publisher. Therefore, if the negotiation of the translation price fails, or even if the foreign publisher simply refuses to accept the translation, preferring to work his own (which is highly improbable), you should continue with the deal. You may, if you choose, pay the translator from the advance you receive after signing the contract. The reason for this is the same as above, namely that this buyer may be the only one interested in your title. Of course, you may remain firm in your terms if you have two or more potential buyers.

Once the major provisions of the deal have been determined, either you or your attorney will prepare the legal document including language and territories granted, all financial and temporal terms, exclusivity or non-exclusivity, duration of the contract, sales reports, currency in which payments will be made, any subsidiary rights granted (electronic version, serialization, excerpts, movie, and others), and copyright notices. The contract may be either a two-party or a three-party contract, depending on whether the translator-agent is included in the stipulations of the contract. Even though you conduct transactions with the translator-agent via a separate contract, this person may also be included in the licensing contract, with additional obligations such as post-contractual communication with the buying publisher and mediation in any payment issues which might arise.

A model of the contract for licensing translation rights appears in the *Appendices* section of this book.

All communication and negotiation of the deal takes place between the Foreign Rights or Copyright departments of the two publishers, between the manager and either of those departments, or between the managers themselves. You should send a signed copy to the buying publisher, who will then remit a countersigned copy.

One note of caution remains: You are strongly urged not to sign a foreign publisher's contract, especially without its having been reviewed by an attorney, unless it is written in a widely spoken language with all wording clear and unambiguous.

These are the basic elements of the pre-deal and negotiation stages of a licensing translation rights transaction. For more advanced learning and additional details, you are encouraged to consult the literature dedicated to this subject. This book focuses on the translator-agent system, the practice of which will result in more opportunities for such deals.

Translators

Working as a freelance translator comes close to being a perfect job for many people with an interest and aptitude in languages. Not only can they use the linguistic skills they have developed and doubtless enjoy, but they can work as many or as few hours as they choose, scheduling work around other commitments when necessary.

With the advent of the internet, translation opportunities have expanded exponentially, making it possible to locate, work on, communicate about, and complete translation projects around the world in days rather than months.

Furthermore, a freelance translator can usually choose which projects to work on, whether limiting them to a certain field of expertise such as mathematics or scientific inquiry, or including the broader range of short fiction, novels, and magazine articles.

Some work entirely on academic projects such as textbooks and foreign language learning; others may work as part of a group of translators on huge government or technical enterprises. Often the freelance translator can set the desired fee for his work, either by placing a bid for the job or negotiating with the owner of the title under translation.

Translators represent a wide cross-section of the population in terms of age, education, experience, interests, and ability. Along with the obvious requirement to know well the original and target languages, it is equally important to have an intuitive ability to communicate.

The translator must understand the difference between a literal translation and the actual message the author wishes to convey – between denotation and connotation – and have sufficient facility with the target language to choose between these options when necessary.

The standard translation job has a fixed time limit and a fixed payment amount. The employer states these parameters in the job post, and only translators who can accept those terms will apply. Freelancers, on the other hand, tend to look for non-standard projects which will provide a steady source of income as well as the potential for ongoing collaboration. For example, a competent translator who completes a book translation in a timely manner can anticipate further contact from the same publisher for future translation projects.

As a freelancer, you have the opportunity to work translations that match your specialization or field of expertise, your style, and your preferred literary genre. The reasons are obvious: working with material you enjoy and understand is easier and more pleasant than working a text beyond your experience and capability, not to mention that the work on such a text goes much faster than on one which is incomprehensible to you.

It follows, then, that the ideal project is one which fits your interest, knowledge, and literary experience; such a job also generates both immediate and future income, offers further opportunity for collaboration with the employer, and is challenging – even exciting – for you. Such a project can easily be found in the translation market; it is known as the translator-agent system, and is described at length in the chapter titled *The Basic Description of the System*.

Applying for the Job

The freelance translator who wants to search for translator-agent opportunities has several potential avenues to explore. Ads and projects will, of course, be posted on translation marketplace websites and even on regular job websites. In addition, threads in translator forums may contain such hiring announcements. To help identify this type of job among the listings, you should try keywords such as "translator-agent," "translator-agents," "translator agent," "translation rights," "translation and marketing," "book translation," "book translation and marketing," "translation rights marketing," and "licensing translation rights." However, the most productive sites, those where you can find a number of jobs from which to choose according to your preferences, are the web platforms dedicated to the translator-agent system. On such platforms, all of the jobs posted are of this type, and the interface, having the capacity to do a filtered search. allows a quick view of the key elements of each job. On these sites can also be found information about the translator-agent system as well as tips for this kind of job. Such websites can be found by doing a Google search using keywords "translator-agent," "translator-agent jobs," and similar terms.

Before applying for a translator-agent job, you will need to be sure the job is suitable for your profile. The following factors should be considered: first, your native language and location must match the target language and the territory where the title will be sold; second, the title to be translated should correspond to your experience and fields of expertise, including your style and preferred literary genre; and third, the financial conditions set forth in the job ad must meet your needs. (If you meet the employer's other criteria, you may be given the opportunity to negotiate the financial package.) Having located a list of available projects, you should then narrow the search by first selecting a group of ads that match one or two of the elements of your profile (for example, the native language and location). You should then carefully read each ad to see whether one of them meets all criteria, making it the right job.

In addition to the job's compatibility with your own requirements, it is recommended that before actually applying, you do a quick evaluation of the potential for the title in that specific territory. Publishers recognize, of course, that a book which is successful in its country of origin might not enjoy that same success in another locale. Factors to be considered include whether the content is universal, whether the subject is available yet in the target language, whether this is a time-sensitive book, and whether the page count will increase or decrease significantly after translation. It is likely, of course, that the original publisher has already studied these factors and decided that the book does have sales potential in that territory, since he has posted the project for that language. However, you as a resident of that country might have additional information that the publisher didn't know when evaluating the potential of the title, and thus you might decide against the title's salability. If your evaluation of the title's potential is favorable, then the next step is to apply for that job.

When applying for a translator-agent job, you should approach the process as you would any other job application: the point is to gain the attention and confidence of the employer by submitting the most favorable data available. Naturally this does not imply fabrication of details about yourself. In fact, such a distortion of fact would most likely be discovered sooner or later by the employer, raising further questions your suitability.

The first rule for applying for any job is to observe to the letter the requests stated in the publisher's ad regarding the mode of application and the form of communication he prefers. In other words, if the ad specifies a complete résumé formatted in Microsoft Word and sent as an attachment to an e-mail, then that is exactly what you should send. It is also important to send all documents requested. Finally, you should be sure you meet all mandatory requirements mentioned in the ad.

Since the résumé is necessary in all applications, we shall take time here to discuss its content. You must prepare the résumé carefully in the language of the publisher. The job post may, in fact, specify the language of the résumé. It should present your educational background (both high school and college or university), degree(s) obtained, work experience both in direct translating and in tangential experience. For example, the résumé may include not only your translation of a recent novel into French, but also your teaching experience in a French classroom, since both endeavors reveal your facility with the French language. Other fields of expertise – for example, computer programming or musicology – should be included, along with the way such expertise was acquired. Additionally, the resume should mention any skills and experience you have in public relations or sales, or collaborations of any kind with local publishers, as these skills will enhance the "agent" activity of a translator-agent.

It is recommended that you do not edit a single general résumé to be sent to all employers, but instead, each résumé should be tailored to the specific requirements of the job for which it is intended. The translator who takes the time to customize his résumé will favorably impress an employer as an individual who cares about this particular job; in other words, he will not view this application as just one of a mass-mailing of identical résumés saturating the market.

If the résumé is accompanied by a letter of intention (cover letter), the letter should describe briefly how your education and fields of expertise relate to the job in question and the title to be translated. It should also focus on the agent activity as well as the translation. In a few words, the letter should explain to the publisher why you consider yourself the best person for his posted job. The cover letter, as a general rule, should not exceed one page in length.

Finally, you must exercise extreme care in preparing the résumé and letter. The translation should be perfect, and these documents should contain no errors in formatting, spelling, grammar, or even typographical mistakes. Needless to say, the composition, editing, and proofreading must be flawless. After all, these documents provide the publisher with the first sample of your skill and thus, your qualification for the job. Samples of different résumé formats may be found on various internet sites using the keyword "résumé" or "résumé format."

Of course you may apply simultaneously for several jobs, depending upon your specialization and skills. Then you may either choose from among those offered, or time permitting, you may even work two jobs at once.

Relationship with the Original Publisher Before Starting the Activity

Through the application process, the hiring publisher will have narrowed his selection and held more extensive discussions with those applicants who seem most promising. He will have made his selection and informed you, and you have presumably accepted his offer with all conditions set forth. The next step in the relationship between you and the hiring publisher is a round of discussions via e-mail or telephone to clarify all points of the contract. These discussions, it should be noted, are to be conducted in the language of the publisher. This point is important because it is essential that you feel comfortable communicating in the original publisher's language as well as your own native language. These initial communications provide the opportunity for you to clear up any confusion and raise any questions you might have concerning the translator-agent system. The hiring publisher will provide informational materials for you and will remain at your disposal to answer any questions that may arise as you study the materials. This time of learning, questioning, and discussing allows both of you to become comfortable with each other's style of communicating, so that you will not hesitate to approach the publisher with any questions that arise later in your collaboration.

The next round of discussions will take the form of negotiations. If some elements of the deal were stated as negotiable, now is the time for these negotiations. You may negotiate the fee for the translation work, the publisher's guarantees, and the agent's commission, as well as the deadlines for the upcoming work – of which there are two: the deadline for completing and delivering the translation itself, and the deadline for finding a buyer for the translation rights.

Regarding the translation fee, which usually is expressed per 300-word page or per word, our recommendation is that you ask a fee somewhat lower than your usual fee because the conditions of this type of job are different from those in a standard translation project. For one thing, if the translation rights sell, you will receive not only your translation fee, but also the ongoing agent commission. If they don't sell, you may recover part of the translation fee and/or may earn co-author royalties in case the selling publisher produces the foreign edition himself. (This contingency may be covered as part of the guarantees offered by the hiring publisher.) And of course not to be discounted are the intangible benefits of this type of job, namely the prestigious addition to your portfolio and the potential for future collaborations with all of the publishers with whom you come in contact as part of the agent's activity. Of course, the risk of not selling the translation rights remains, and you should weigh that risk according to your criteria and needs. This risk is an element that you should bring up when negotiating. The recommendation to lower the translation fee is based upon the assumption that the hiring publisher has a reserve of applicants from which to choose; therefore, if you set the fee too high, or are too insistent upon the figure you have requested, the publisher may simply terminate the relationship and offer the job to the next person on the list.

When negotiating guarantees, you should be aware that the publisher will probably be less flexible. Even though the translation fee is not actually paid by the original publisher, the guarantees involve costs only he can cover, and the outcome of these discussions, therefore, depends directly upon the publisher's budget.

The agent's commission is the financial element that should present the least concern to you. The reason for this is that once you find a buyer, your income is assured – that is, the translation fee plus a regular commission in whatever amount is agreed upon. Therefore, in negotiations on this subject, you should not be too insistent, saving your resources for negotiating the other elements.

The last point of negotiation is the deadlines. These dates are even more important than the financial agreements. As mentioned earlier, there are two deadlines that will concern you: the date for delivery of the translation to the publisher, and the deadline for finding a buying publisher. The time needed for the translation will depend not only upon the difficulty of the text, but also on your other professional and personal commitments. For a difficult text, you should not accept a deadline that is too early, because rushing such a translation could result in errors, or simply in a lower quality of work.

The deadline for finding a buyer for the translated title should be chosen according to the number of publishers in the target country or territory. You would be wise to look through local directories of publishers prior to negotiations so as to have an idea of the number of publishers you will need to contact. (See also the section titled *Database* in the sub-chapter *Marketing the Translation Rights*.) The number of publishers that you must contact will depend upon whether the marketed title is addressed to every publisher in the area, or only to those in a certain specialty. Based upon that number, you should estimate the time needed for making these contacts. From that date forward, you should add one week to collect the first replies, whether positive or negative, another week from the last positive reply for preliminary discussions, an additional month at the minimum for reviewing the book, and one more week for finalizing the discussions. Generally, six months should be enough time to complete the campaign in a medium-sized country. Thus, you should not accept an earlier deadline for finding a buyer; after all, it is in the publisher's best interest as well as your own to conduct a thorough and efficient sales campaign. Even so, the publisher may push for an earlier deadline than is advisable or even realistic, and you must hold steadfast in negotiating your side. Weighing all risks and benefits, and knowing when to be flexible and when to remain firm will result in a good deal all the way around.

In the next round of communications, you and the hiring publisher will complete and sign a contract. The publisher will send you a contract draft via e-mail or postal mail (requiring two copies), based upon what both parties agreed to in negotiations. You or your attorney must read the draft carefully, every clause of it, to be sure it contains all of the obligations and rights of both parties, especially in regard to terms of payment. If either party finds errors or misrepresentations, these should be cleared up immediately and a new draft prepared. However, if everything is correct and matches the prior agreement, you should sign two copies and remit them to the publisher, who will then return a countersigned copy to you. From this moment, the relationship is official and you may start working the translation.

In the meantime, the publisher will provide you with a letter of introduction, verifying that you are his representative acting in his behalf in the respective territory. You should carry this letter at all times when approaching the local publishers in person as they may ask for identification. Along with this letter, the publisher may send other marketing materials such as a presentation letter to accompany the title you are representing, a title description, any pertinent marketing data, and so on. These materials may arrive after you have begun the translating work, or even after the translation is complete and the marketing phase has begun.

Both during the translation work and after it is completed, the selling publisher will continue training you from a distance. In fact, the training might continue even after the agent activity has begun. It is very important that you take this training seriously and follow the publisher's guidelines exactly, as he is much more knowledgeable and experienced than you might be. If any questions at all arise, or if anything is unclear at any point after you start the agent's campaign, you should not hesitate to ask the publisher for guidance and clarification. From now on, there should, in fact, be ongoing communication between both you and the publisher, most of which will be devoted to training.

Translation

After all details of your collaboration with the publisher have been agreed upon and the contract signed, your first task is to translate the book from its original language into your native language – that is, the language of the country in which you reside – within the time frame you agreed upon with the publisher. This is the project for which you initially applied and the skill you brought with you to the position.

When you applied for this translator-agent job, you also applied for the specific title, which you will now translate, so the assumption is that you are familiar with the topic as well as the style and literary genre of the book; if it is a specialized book, it is also assumed that you hold some expertise in the book's subject.

You should have received as well a sample portion of the text, or perhaps the entire text, from the hiring publisher during the preliminary rounds of discussion; therefore, you are at least somewhat familiar with the text, and the translation work should go smoothly from beginning to end. Nevertheless, you may encounter some words and phrases whose meaning is unclear, and here is where the intuitive ability to communicate will be helpful. You will need to deduce the author's intent in the passage before you can accurately translate it. This situation can occur when the author of the original text was not writing in his native language. (Publishers do sometimes carry authors who are not native to the language in which they write.)

The best way to approach such a circumstance is simply to remain in continual contact with the publisher during your translation work and ask for additional support such as explanations, definitions, rephrasing, and the like for every unclear meaning. For example, the Romanian adjective *remanent* has no literal English translation. In order to correctly translate that term, you need to ask the publisher what he wants to say here. (This term is surprisingly similar to the English noun *remnant* which means 'a remaining portion' and in fact, does have a similar meaning: 'a continuing or ongoing element.') Later in this chapter, we will cover some specific translation problems.

It is recommended that you work the translation directly on the original source document, replacing the original text progressively with the translated one. This way, you will save time and preserve the original design of the document, and when you have finished, the publisher will receive a print-ready copy needing only minor adjustments.

The publisher will supply an editable document of the book's content immediately after signing the contract. He will also provide clear instructions as to how to approach the technical editing of the translation. Additionally, he will train you about the translation itself, and you must follow his directions exactly. Bear in mind that he knows more about this text than you do. You must translate exactly what you have, with no additions or omissions of information, even if you consider them necessary in some places. For example, since you are presumably working on material with which you have some expertise, you may wish to provide information the author has omitted. Or you may think the text is unnecessarily wordy and attempt to pare it down. Neither of these alterations is acceptable; you are to translate the text as you have it. It is good to remember also that you are legally bound by the warranty of translation clause in the contract.

Of course, it will occasionally be necessary to change wording somewhat in order to convey the appropriate meaning given the culture and the language of the translation. For instance, consider an idiomatic usage in English, "to get your goat." To an American English speaker, this means to do something which is intended to annoy someone. If you are unaware of this idiom, you might translate it literally and distort the author's meaning – especially if the text has nothing to do with ungulates! Mistranslations of idioms, semantic variants, and terms that are "untranslatable" can result in humorous or even embarrassing errors. In some cases, the outcome could be offensive or even dangerous. In one case, the American name of a popular cooking oil translated into an insulting term in the target language. In another instance, a street sign in Wales advised pedestrians to "look left" to avoid oncoming traffic. The word translated as "left" in fact means "right" – clearly a potentially perilous error. A Google search of "translation errors" lists over 2.5 million such entries, so mistranslation is a frequent problem.

Translation software, while it might seem to be a panacea, especially if the text is long and difficult, should be used with care. If you use such software, you must still review the document carefully to be sure the correct meanings have been conveyed. To cite just one example, a recent study showed that medicine labels translated from English into Spanish by pharmaceutical translation software yielded errors on fifty percent of the labels, errors which could have resulted in harm to the patient.

Keep in mind that typographical spelling errors may actually result in translational errors. Again we use an example from the English language: *lose*, a verb meaning 'to misplace' or 'to have something taken away' is frequently misspelled "loose," which means 'uncontrolled' or 'not fastened tightly.' Every language has such words, and you must proofread very carefully to be sure that you have not committed such inaccuracies. You have been hired under the assumption that you will not make such errors; therefore, do not hesitate to ask the publisher for clarification on any wording that you do not understand.

Let us consider now how to manage your time so that you meet the deadline stated in the contract. It is recommended that you work a portion each day, perhaps dividing the number of pages by the number of days available to you to complete the translation. In this way, a 500-page book with a deadline date two months away would require you to do between eight and nine pages a day. It is better to spread your work out evenly than to try to complete a large portion at once, and then wait a week or two to do another large section. Working sporadically in this manner can cause you to lose your train of thought and you will find yourself needing to review sections worked earlier – which takes extra time – in order to maintain continuity in your thought as you work the translation.

After finishing each day's work, you should read over the translated text from that day, making any necessary changes and corrections, including typographical errors, and format that section in its final form according to the publisher's instructions. Needless to say, you must do software spelling checks if possible. But be cautious in using spell-checking and grammar-checking software. After all, you know what the text should say, and the software does not. As an example, earlier in this chapter, the phrase "the book's content" was tagged by the grammar-checker. While the possessive form for an inanimate object is unusual, it is not incorrect; moreover, if the author had substituted the suggested phrase "books are," the phrase would have made no sense – and ironically, would have been grammatically incorrect.

As you approach the agreed-upon deadline, if you find that you will not be able to complete the translation, you must contact the publisher and request an extension of the deadline. He will surely understand that the reasons for your request are related solely to translation issues, and the two of you will agree on a new deadline for delivery of the translation.

Marketing the Translation Rights

The "agent" portion of this job that you have accepted is not much different from the customary literary agent or agency. The elements that are missing from a standard agent's activity are negotiations between the buying publisher and the selling publisher, arrangement of contract signing between the two publishers, monitoring the flow of the collaboration based on the contract, collecting payments, and mediating payment disputes.

Once you have found a publisher interested in buying the translation rights to this title, the selling publisher will take over the process and finalize the deal. The reason for this approach is that even though you have functioned as an agent up to this point, you probably lack the experience that a conventional agent has in carrying out these tasks. Moreover, since your primary expertise is in translation, you will want to devote your time to that pursuit rather than spending effort on new activities for which you are not trained and which eventually might become unpleasant for you.

Even though you will pass the above tasks to the selling publisher, you may still be involved in the licensing the rights if you wish. As you have probably realized by now, some of those tasks may affect you: for example, payment disputes could have an impact on your future commissions. Therefore, your involvement in mediation of unsatisfactory payments may persuade the buying publisher to pay what is due so that the selling publisher will more quickly receive the royalties, and consequently you will receive your commissions sooner.

The first stage of the marketing process – contacting the publishers and presenting them with the offer – is the standard protocol for all agents. Therefore, at this stage, you will be doing the same thing as any other agent. This activity is not at all difficult. It simply requires communication with the publishers on your list, and with the support of your selling publisher, you can accomplish this part smoothly and efficiently. What you have to offer that the selling publisher probably lacks is your ability to communicate in your native language with publishers in your area.

There is nothing so far that a standard literary agent does that you cannot do. The only real difference between you and the classical agent is a relationship portfolio the he uses in any sales campaign and a sales portfolio that serves as his credentials. You will acquire both of these in due course. After your first successful sales campaign, you will have developed relationships with local publishers as well as a sale, and thus over time, you will slowly build your own portfolios to help you in your future marketing.

However, you *do* have something that a standard agent usually does not have, and that is a completed translation of the book. The publisher buying your title will thus be spared the time-consuming tasks of finding a translator, conducting negotiations with that individual, and then waiting until the work is complete before moving forward with the book. This is no small advantage and will compensate to a great extent for the absence of portfolios.

Even though the marketing activity does not require solicitation and does not involve particular skills other than the ability to approach and communicate well with people, it does require some basic training that the publisher will supply. So once again, we stress the importance of following exactly the instructions of the hiring publisher and asking for guidance at any time questions or issues arise related to your marketing activity.

The first step of this marketing campaign is for you to create a database – a list of publishers that you will approach, along with their contact information.

Database

The list of publisher contacts you are about to make should take the form of a database with several fields: name of the publisher, main specialty (technical books, novels, etc.), e-mail address, telephone number, postal and web addresses, contact information of specific departments dealing with translation rights (Foreign Rights, Copyright, Production), dates when contacted, and dates when replies are received.

An Excel spreadsheet will work nicely for such a database, though you may have another program that you prefer. In an Excel file, the new entries are easy to insert and edit, and you also have search options available if you need filtered results.

Depending on the topic of the title you are marketing, you may include only the local publishers of certain specialties, or you may list all publishers. Some titles address only certain topics and a general publisher or a publisher of a different specialty will not likely be interested in publishing them. For example, a novel will not interest an exclusively technical publisher. Likewise, scientific or academic books are unlikely to capture the attention of a publisher whose specialty is how-to guides or gardening; for that matter, even a general publisher who is small or medium-sized may lack the resources to handle a book of that genre. However, such books may well be of interest to large publishers who have a scientific imprint or an academic division.

Even with these considerations, it is recommended that you eventually complete a database listing all publishers in your country, as you may use it for future licensing-translation-rights campaigns as well as other projects.

However, compiling an extensive list might require substantial time – time that you could be using to complete a sale – so it is recommended that you begin with publishers for the specialty of your current campaign, and then as you have time, and after you have completed this campaign, you can continue to increase your database.

Bear in mind that a complete database could take anywhere from weeks to months to complete, depending upon the size of your country and its specific economic environment, factors which determine the number of publishers on your list. One possibility, of course, if you expect to include a very large number of entries, is to prepare your database in a shorter form – that is, with fewer fields.

While there is no one specific formula for completing your database, you need to organize your list efficiently so as to avoid wasting time or including double entries.

Sources where you can find the information you need to build your database will include local business directories, both publishers' and general directories, some printed and others online.

You can also search the *Publishers* category in the local Yellow Pages, which has both printed and online formats. This source lists a large number of local publishers, but provides very little other information – essentially their physical addresses, e-mail, and telephone numbers. Their specialties are not indicated. You can, however, visit their websites and collect further information from there.

You might also find other, smaller, local business directories where you can find information in the same *Publishers* category. Many of these directories are available in print form at larger public libraries where there is no cost for you to use them; they are also, of course, available for purchase.

The best source – that is, the source providing the most information per entry – is a directory specifically dedicated to the book industry (publishers, agents, distributors, bookstores). Directories of this kind are to be found mostly on the internet rather than in print form, and you can locate them by searching keywords "publishers directory," "book industry directory," and "publishers." Of course you will enter these search terms in your own language. In these directories, you will usually find the specialties of the listed publishers; if the specialties are not included, you can find the specialty of a publisher by visiting his website, which is probably included in directories of this type. From that website, you can often get the contact information for specific departments which deal with translation rights.

You may begin contacting publishers when your database is complete, or even during its construction. This latter option is recommended if you anticipate a large number of listings that will take too long to complete. In this case, you might contact several publishers daily – for example, those newly added to your list each day.

In order to keep your database well organized, you should update it every time you send a message or make a telephone call, and every time you receive a response. Be sure to enter the date of these contacts. To do this, you must include fields (columns in Excel) for dates of messages sent and replies received.
For example, you would include a field (or column) labeled *Message 1* followed by a field labeled *Reply 1*, then *Message 2* and *Reply 2,* and so on. Then, when you send your first message to a publisher, you should note the date of that contact under *Message 1* in that publisher's row; later, when you receive a reply from him, you will note that date in the *Reply 1* field.

At the minimum, your database should be updated daily with all new listings you have acquired and all messages and replies generated. You can readily see how this method will be useful when you have a great many messages and replies to manage in your marketing campaign.

In the next section, you will find more information about contacting publishers.

Contacting Publishers

As the translator-agent, you are the one who will establish and conduct the entire flow of communication with local publishers. The approach you choose for each individual publisher will depend upon your experience as well as your acquaintance with the publisher and the size of the publishing house, among other factors. As an example, a small publisher with whom you have worked previously will probably call for a less formal approach than a larger company or one requiring introductions before presenting the book you are marketing.

In any case, the first thing to consider is the order in which you will contact these publishers. One method, maybe the simplest, is just to begin at the top of your database and go down your list, in the order you have arranged them, contacting a certain number of individuals each day. However, we recommend that your first contacts include any publishers with whom you have had prior contact or collaboration. If you have a large number of potential contacts, however, you will probably also want to filter your database according to the publishers' specialties, and work first with those whose specialty matches your title.

The reason for prioritizing your contact list this way (first, those you know and/or those whose specialty matches your title) is that from these two groups, you are more likely to get a positive response, or at least an earlier one. Since your ultimate goal is to find a buyer for the translation rights, contacting the above group(s) first increases the likelihood of a quicker sale. If the book you are marketing does not address a specialty, you can move down your contact database, still giving priority to those publishers with whom you have dealt in the past.

The second consideration is the form of communication you will use. E-mail, postal letter, telephone calls, and personal meetings are all acceptable approaches; this decision depends entirely upon your personal preferences and criteria, which of course include cost. E-mail, while essentially free, is a less formal approach. The classical postal letter is always correct, but may be more costly in the long run, especially if you have a long list of contacts. It is also more time-consuming. Telephone calls may or may not cost a great deal, depending on the locations and your long-distance telephone plan. Another possibility is a personal meeting with some of the publishers. Let us look further at the advantages and disadvantages of each method.

    E-mail is probably the most efficient in terms of time and cost. You have to compose only one message (perhaps with slight variances to suit individual contacts). However, if you choose this method, it is recommended that you send the messages one by one, rather than as bulk mail (that is, placing several addresses in the "To," "CC," or "BCC" fields). Many e-mail clients and programs automatically move bulk mail messages into a "Spam" or "Junk" folder and they do not reach their intended recipients. Besides this concern, larger publishers may ignore your email or simply forget to reply.

    The formal letter, sent by post, is the standard approach; however, it involves higher cost, as it entails the price of paper, printing, and postage. This method is also more time-consuming, not only in terms of preparation, but also because mail delivery takes anywhere from two days to as much as ten days to reach the addressee. Still, this approach may be more effective for large publishers. If you choose to send letters, we suggest you send them as "Priority Mail." Not only does a "Priority" envelope catch the attention of the recipient, but you also have the option of confirming its delivery with the post office.

    Telephone calls should probably be used as a first contact only when you have had prior collaboration with the publisher. A telephone call by its nature requires an immediate response, and will most likely result in a "call-back" since the person you are calling will need time to consider his reply.

Our recommendation is to take a double-contact approach: use e-mail or a letter for your first message, and then follow up with a telephone call a few days later. The body of your message might even contain the clause "I will telephone you early next week to be sure you have received this message" or something similar.

Personal meetings as an initial method of contact are not recommended; however, you may arrange personal meetings with publishers from whom you receive positive responses after your first e-mail or letter. Some will request more details or samples, and in time, one or more will declare their intention to buy the rights. Of course in any case, courtesy demands that you telephone or e-mail ahead to arrange an appointment.

Unlike the other contact methods, however, the personal meeting requires great attention to your personal appearance and demeanor, as well as to the message you will deliver. Since you will almost certainly meet with the publisher in person eventually, especially if further collaborations ensue from your initial contact, you should keep several points in mind.

The guidelines for a personal meeting are the same as for any business meeting. You should dress conservatively and appropriately. For men, this usually means neatly pressed dress slacks, long-sleeved shirt, tie, and coordinating jacket. A three-piece suit is probably a bit too imposing, however. For women, a stylish but conservative suit or coordinated outfit is recommended. Remember that you are not there to impress the publisher with your high-fashion style, but with your good judgment of what he will want to purchase.

You should plan ahead what you want to say to the publisher, and if you don't have a lot of experience, it might be wise to rehearse by yourself beforehand. Do not, however, try to memorize a "script"; you will sound uncomfortable, and if you should forget the speech you had prepared, you will flounder about and lose confidence. It is best to know your subject well (as of course you will, since you did the translation) and be able to discuss your product and answer the publisher's questions in a professional and intelligent manner.

Be sure to carry with you all of the presentation materials that the selling publisher gave you, including your letter of introduction or other personal credentials to verify that you speak for the selling publisher. These should be well organized in the order you expect to present them, so you do not have to scramble through your briefcase in search of a document or form you need.

You should talk with the general manager or the manager of a department that deals with translation rights, or with the person with whom the appointment was made. Begin by introducing yourself not only as the translator of the marketed book, but also as the selling publisher's representative in that country, acting in his behalf.

The foregoing discussion gives an overview of your initial contacts with publishers. We now want to look more closely at the first message; whether e-mail or postal letter, it should meet the following requirements:

- The letter or message should be succinct. Publishers do not like long messages, so yours might be deleted or discarded without being read entirely.
- It should introduce you as a representative of the original publisher and translator and agent on behalf of the original publisher. This creates a stronger favorable impression of the company you represent.
- The message should contain a "hook" – that is, a surprising detail that will quickly capture the recipient's attention and make him want to read further. The fact that another publisher's translator is contacting him is already a surprising element. You will want to add a phrase such as "print-ready translation," "publish a translation in days," or "translation rights for our best-seller" if that is true of the marketed title.

- Your letter should put forward briefly but clearly the title and the offer. You should make your presentation around the key elements of content novelties, good reviews, sales potential, and other published foreign editions (if any). Also mention again that the translation is already done.
- You should ask for permission to send further details and samples of the translation as well as a review copy of the original book.
- This initial letter should not discuss financial terms. These will be addressed in future messages or meetings.
- Finally, be sure to include your own contact information (name, e-mail address, telephone number) as well as that of the selling publisher.

A note of caution: Never attach any samples when sending your first message to a publisher. Not only could your message end up in the recipient's spam folder before he sees it, but doing so might violate the publisher's rules for submission. In either case, your action will have a negative outcome.

Next is a model of a first message that meets the above requirements.

Addressing, introducing	Dear Sir or Madame: My name is [*your name*] and I represent [*the selling publisher's name*] as translator and translation rights agent for [*your country*].
Hooking attention	Please allow me to present you a title with good potential for [*your country*] for which we are currently conducting a local marketing campaign to license the [*your native language*] rights. We already have the translation completed, and thus you can publish the book within a matter of days.

Brief presentation of the title	[*original title of the marketed book*] was published in [*year of publishing*] and made [*mention some sales statistics, if favorable; also, relevant reviews*]. The book is about [*the topic and subject of the book*], which is of great interest nowadays in [*mention some territories including your country*], due to [*mention a reason*]. Compared with other similar titles on the market, ours has [*mention key elements of the content that makes it different, novelties brought, etc.*].
Brief presentation of the offer	As I also hold expertise in [*your fields of expertise related to book's topic*] we can provide you with a professional and accurate translation, already completed and edited with all the graphics. If we reach agreement on your purchase of translation rights, we can provide you also with the original cover editable file. Terms of licensing the rights remain entirely negotiable.
Asking for permission	If this title interests you, please do not hesitate to contact me for additional details. In completion of this presentation, please allow me to send you a sample of the translation and a review copy of the original book upon receipt of your request.
Closing formula and contact data	Thank you for your time. I look forward to your early reply. Best regards, [*your name*] [*your e-mail address*] [*your phone*] [*the selling publisher's name*] [*a selling publisher's e-mail address*] [*the selling publisher's website address*]

Of course, the message composition itself will depend on the title you are marketing, as each title has its own particular attributes that should be mentioned. If you are marketing several titles at once, you should mention all of them, keeping their presentations brief so that your letter doesn't become too long. The selling publisher will probably have provided you with already edited message models, or at least with the relevant data that should be included in the initial message.

Subsequent messages sent to this particular publisher should take the form of replies to his questions and requests for further details. Never send the same message twice while waiting for a reply; such repetition becomes spam and has a negative impact on your campaign. In fact, your impatience could result in termination of contact altogether with this publisher.

If your first message aroused the publisher's interest in the title, he will get back to you and a round of discussions will follow about the title, the translation, and the terms of the potential deal. Such discussion may take place in two or three messages or in an actual personal meeting. If you do not hear back from that publisher, then he is definitely not interested in your offer, and you should not contact him again about this title.

Be sure at this point to update your database to reflect these contacts and replies, noting their dates in the respective fields, so that you do not inadvertently contact a publisher twice with the same message. Regular and consistent updating also helps to keep your correspondence organized. As your list of contacts grows, you will almost certainly forget whom you e-mailed, who replied to your first message, who replied to the second, and so on, and therefore, good organization is a must.

In the forthcoming discussions, you will be asked to send samples and to state the financial terms of the deal that the selling publisher is offering. Your presentation of these materials and terms must follow the selling publisher's instructions, stating that the terms are negotiable directly with the selling publisher after the foreign publisher has reviewed the samples.

Typically, you will provide a partial translation sample (a PDF file containing roughly ninety percent of the content, as a basic protection against copyright theft) and a physical copy of the original book (not a translation) which the selling publisher should have sent to you before starting the campaign. When you send the samples, ask the publisher how much time he needs to review these materials, and make a note to follow up in the time frame he has requested. Meanwhile, continue the contact process with other publishers on your list.

When the review period for a publisher draws to an end, contact him again asking for his opinion and intention. If he did not state a required reviewing time, do not wait incessantly for his feedback, but allow at least two to three weeks from the date he received the materials before contacting him again.

When a publisher eventually decides to buy the translation rights, you should immediately do the following:

- Inform the buying publisher that from this point forward, he will be communicating directly with the selling publisher who will contact him soon.
- Inform the selling publisher of the imminent deal and provide him with the contact information of the buying publisher.
- Stop contacting new publishers and answer only the replies you receive, adding that discussions are already underway with a local publisher who wishes to acquire the translation rights. Keep in mind, however, that the deal is not closed until a contract is signed, so you must remain available and do not ignore other interested publishers.

Most of the guidelines and recommendations presented in this section will probably be included in the training that the selling publisher provides as you prepare for this marketing campaign. That training is specific to each publisher and also depends on the particularities of each marketed title.

If your deadline for finding a buyer approaches with no success, you should ask the selling publisher for an extension as in the case of the translation deadline. Since both of you are interested in find a buyer, you will in all probability arrive at a new deadline agreement. However, if you do pass the newer deadline without a sale, the clauses of your contract which cover this situation come into effect. In this case, according to what is stipulated there, your collaboration with the selling publisher may end and you will be paid for the portion of the translation fee covered by the guarantees you initially received with no further rights to the work (except intellectual rights, which remain yours). Also, you may continue if your contract and/or guarantees specify that you will receive royalties on a future edition in that foreign language published by that selling publisher. For more information on this contingency, see the *Guarantees* section in *Publishers* chapter.

After Finding a Buying Publisher

Once a foreign publisher has declared his intention to purchase the translation rights, both the buying publisher and the selling publisher must reach an agreement on the negotiated terms and sign a contract. At that point, all parties may consider the sale completed. We now enter the post-contractual collaboration.

The translator-agent has at this point accomplished his contractual task and may now return to his other projects. If he wishes, he may apply later for other translator-agent jobs offered by the same publisher or by a different one. A good reason for choosing the latter is that he has now developed a complete local publisher database, gained experience and skills, and also now holds a portfolio of sales (albeit only one sale) and a relationship portfolio, all of which he may use again. When applying to a different publisher, he should be sure to update his résumé to include this most recent sale.

Depending on the stipulations of the translator-agent's contract with the hiring publisher, as well as his own preference, he may become involved in closely monitoring the flow of the post-contractual relationship between the two publishers, especially with respect to terms and payment obligations. As noted earlier, the translator-agent's compensation for agent activity may be directly affected by the collaboration now underway.

After the contract for licensing rights expires (usually a period of three to seven years), the translator-agent may be approached again by the selling publisher to renew the contract with the buying publisher. If that publisher is not interested in an extension of the licensing rights, the translator-agent may be asked to find another interested local publisher.

Finding a buyer for a translated title in no way signals the end of the selling publisher's work; on the contrary, he must at this point become fully engaged with the buying publisher, taking over from his translator-agent all communication with the buying publisher both before and after signing the contract.

Post-contractual collaboration between the two publishers follows the standard protocol for licensing translation rights; the most important thing is to be sure that the terms of the contract are being observed with regard to the publishing date, the first print run, the date of payment of the advance, and then the payment of the regular royalties. The two publishers are now in effect working in partnership and therefore, the selling publisher should provide as much support as needed for the buying publisher with regard to editing and publishing the foreign edition. This help will include supplying him with all editable files (including the cover file) that will make his work easier. He should also offer any marketing tips that he has specific to that title. All parties concerned will benefit from an accommodating relationship between the two publishers.

Once the translation rights to a title are sold in a foreign country, this fact should be included as a key element when conducting any future marketing campaigns for this title in other countries. Therefore, the selling publisher should update the materials he provides to the next translator-agent in another country. Since any publisher will want to be among the first to offer a best-seller, the news that this title has already sold successfully in another country will be an asset to the agent marketing the title.

Summary and Comments

The translator-agent system we have proposed and described in this book was not invented and developed by an individual or a company, but has arisen as an inevitable consequence of globalization in the book industry – as well as the law of supply and demand which governs this industry. For this reason, we do not even pretend that we created the system, nor do we claim a proprietary license on its use. Our purpose is simply to make the system known, to describe its functionality, and to provide support for all who want to adopt it for their use – publishers and translators alike.

Because the system makes perfect sense, it is also quite simple and it works quite easily. Briefly, when the original publisher wishes to market the licensing of translation rights to a title he has published, he first hires a translator who is both native in the language and a resident of the specific country where he wishes to publish, and who specializes in that title's topic, genre, and style. At this point, however, the translator-agent system departs from the traditional method of selling translation rights in that the publisher asks the translator to act also in the capacity of a foreign rights agent, marketing the translation rights for that title to local publishers.

After both the original publisher and the translator agree on terms and sign the contract, the translator-agent begins his double job: first he completes the translation, then he offers it to local publishers through a personal marketing campaign which consists of contacting them and presenting the offer under the auspices of the hiring (original) publisher.

Once the translator-agent has found a buyer for the translation rights, all further transactions for this sale are conducted between the two publishers. After the license contract is signed by both parties and the buying publisher pays for the translation, the translator is paid by the hiring publisher for the translation work plus further commissions from the royalties on the new foreign edition. If, however, the translator-agent fails to find a buyer within the agreed period of time, he may receive payments covered by the guarantees set forth in his contract with the hiring (selling) publisher. These guarantees could include a portion of the translation fee and/or royalties on a future edition published by the original publisher in that foreign language.

This is in essence how the system works. In previous chapters, we have described in detail each element of the system and every step of the process for each party involved, the selling publisher as well as the native translator-agent.

What we have presented in this book is the standard scheme of the translator-agent system; this method can also work with other variations – in fact, each publisher can determine his own system by changing any of the elements or even by adding new elements according to his preferences. Any variations, however, will be based on this standard method. And of course the basic system is always subject to changes and improvements within any of its elements, which is to be expected with any process.

This system also works well for a translation agency working in the role of the translator-agent. In this case, the agency will assign one of its translators to do the actual translation and pay him according to the agency's own policy; then the agency will conduct a marketing campaign using its full range of resources, including personnel. The obvious difference here is that the recipient of any agent commissions and royalties will be the agency itself, not the individual translator.

The translator-agent system is suitable primarily for small and medium-sized publishers because of the relatively minimal outlay of money and resources involved. Of course large publishers will also find the system useful to reach new territories not covered by their agents or simply to try a new approach when the standard method of selling translation rights has produced no positive results.

Besides its obvious applicability for publishing companies large and small, self-published authors can also use this system to their advantage if they have registered their own company as the publishers of their books. Even if they have not done this, self-published authors can still market their books through a translator-agent system, but they will be required to put more effort into the marketing process. For example, even though these self-published books hold an ISBN code, they have no publishing imprint and most likely had low sales in the original edition, so it may be very difficult to convince a foreign publisher that they have good sales potential in that country. Of course, a record of high sales will significantly change this picture.

"Is this system really workable?" one may ask upon first learning about it. The answer is yes. A practical system can be said to be workable in any one of three situations: 1) when all of its components can be procured, arranged according to the system's structure, and put to work easily; 2) when the system is based on natural and proven principles; and 3) when the system has been tested and has resulted in a positive outcome. The translator-agent system meets not one but all three of these criteria.

First, the translator-agent, who is in fact the "engine" of the system, is relatively easy to find, since the translation market is a large one and the supply of available translators exceeds the demand for their services. Therefore, a publisher will always be able to choose from among a number of native translators waiting for new projects. The second criterion, that of a system based on predictable and proven principles, is met in the fact that the entire translator-agent system, from the hiring of the translator-agent to the sale of the translation rights, is based on the principle of supply and demand; furthermore, it uses basic marketing principles and follows proven psychological sales. As for the third criterion, both our publishing house and other publishers and translators worldwide have used this system with positive results.

At this point, we should mention that if a publisher or translator has used the translator-agent system only once and failed to sell a title's translation rights in a particular country, he might be inclined to label the system as unworkable. Needless to say, such a generalization is not correct. As shown through the three arguments in the previous paragraph, the system is workable, and the reader who goes through this book will get confirmation of that fact. Of course, there is always the risk that a given campaign will not end in a sale, because the success of any marketing campaign depends primarily on the product being sold and the quality of its marketing, and secondly on the system through which the campaign is conducted.

No matter how good the marketing might be, and regardless of its sales in the original edition, some titles might simply not sell in certain countries. A political or patriotic title, for example, may sell extremely well in its country of origin, but hold little interest elsewhere; this is why publishers must be very careful in selecting titles to market abroad. There exists the temptation for a publisher to throw his titles in bulk on the market of translation rights, but in doing so he risks loss of time and resources when the titles do not sell well. Conversely, a title with good potential in a certain territory might not reach its buyer because of poor marketing practices of the translator-agent. For this reason, publishers must get intensely involved in training their translator-agents before starting the marketing campaign.

All of these factors are discussed at length in the book and are the elements upon which the success of a campaign ultimately depends. Fortunately, this system also offers a compensation for the possible failure of a campaign: the original publisher still has a good translation of his book which he can publish under his own imprint and distribute through global channels. As for the translator-agent who conducts an unsuccessful marketing campaign, the guarantees offered by the hiring publisher can cover part of his work and even generate further income in the form of royalties on a foreign edition published by the original publisher.

In the chapter titled *The Basic Description of the System*, we discussed the advantages and disadvantages inherent in the translator-agent system and concluded that the only major disadvantage is the possible lack of skill and experience of a translator acting as a foreign rights agent. However, this disadvantage is compensated largely by the fact that the selling publisher has a complete and accurate translation ready before presenting the title to foreign publishers. Moreover, the translator by virtue of his education and professional experience can be assumed to possess a high level of sophistication as well as excellent skills in communication, public relations, and persuasive ability. These are the main requirements for acting as a successful agent, and by this token, the translator can handle the agent activity quite well – in some respects perhaps better than a traditional literary agent – though he will still probably lack some business savvy and of course a portfolio specific to this trade.

The system we propose here in no way diminishes the work of classical literary agents nor the role of international book fairs, and is not intended to replace them in the market. In the actual economic environment of the book industry, such a thing would in fact be impossible since there is currently a wide demand for literary agents, and the book fairs continue to offer a good opportunity for a publisher to sell the translation rights for his titles. Even the publisher who uses the translator-agent system might on occasion appeal to a conventional foreign rights agent if the translator fails to find a buyer, or simply to represent his other titles. In short, the ever-present principle of supply and demand will ensure a market for traditional literary agents for a long time to come.

The distinguishing feature of the translator-agent system is that it is global and multidirectional. While the current market for translation rights is preponderantly from English to all other languages – that is to say, titles published in the United States being sold to the rest of the world – the translator-agent system can link any pair of languages equally by selling the rights of titles published in any country to publishers in any other country. Thus, this system may be the first step toward uniform globalization of this market.

As marketplaces dedicated to the translator-agent system proliferate, so translations will be published all over the world, and all publishers will benefit from equal access to the market of translation rights. This equalization, along with the advent of print-on-demand publishing, will be the main current moving the book industry toward a future of total globalization.

**Infarom created on its website the first platform where publishers can post their translator-agent jobs and translators can apply for them.
It can be found at
www.infarom.com/global_translations.html**

Appendices

Appendix 1 – *Letter of Introduction / ID Card*

Company: [*NAME OF THE HIRING PUBLISHER*]
Address: [*ADDRESS OF THE HIRING PUBLISHER*]
Number of registration: [*NUMBER OF REGISTRATION IN THE LOCAL COMMERCE REGISTRY OF THE HIRING PUBLISHER*]

LETTER OF INTRODUCTION
No. _____ / _____

By the current document, we state that its bearer, Mr./Ms. [*NAME OF THE TRANSLATOR-AGENT*], is our company's translator and representative in [*COUNTRY OF THE TRANSLATOR-AGENT*] and acts in our company's behalf in matter of establishing business contacts, licensing translation rights for our titles, intermediating other publishing deals with local publishers, and monitoring the post-contractual collaborations.

This letter of introduction is valid from [*DATE OF STARTING THE MARKETING ACTIVITY*] to [*THE DEADLINE FOR FINDING A BUYER STATED IN THE CONTRACT OF TRANSLATION AND FOREIGN REPRESENTATION*].

[*NAME OF THE HIRING PUBLISHER*] By: (*SIGNATURE*)	**[*NAME OF THE TRANSLATOR-AGENT*]** By: (*SIGNATURE*)
Name: [*NAME OF THE PUBLISHER'S DULY AUTHORIZED OFFICER*] Title: [*TITLE OF THE PUBLISHER'S DULY AUTHORIZED OFFICER*]	Name: [*NAME OF THE TRANSLATOR-AGENT*]

ID CARD

Company:_____
Address: _____
Registration number: _____

IDENTIFICATION CARD
No. ____ /_____

Mr./Ms. _____
Local representative in _____, translator and foreign rights agent.

Valid through _____

Appendix 2 – *Contract of Translation and Foreign Representation*

CONTRACT OF TRANSLATION
AND FOREIGN REPRESENTATION

CONTRACT made this [DATE] (hereinafter referred to as "Effective Date") between [HIRING PUBLISHER'S NAME] of [HIRING PUBLISHER'S ADDRESS] (hereinafter referred to as the "Publisher"], and [TRANSLATOR'S NAME] of [COUNTRY OF THE TRANSLATOR] (hereinafter referred to as the "Translator-Agent"), with his mailing address as [MAILING ADDRESS OF THE TRANSLATOR]:

WHEREAS the Publisher is the sole and exclusive owner of the rights which are the subject of this contract; and

WHEREAS the Translator commits to do the translation into [LANGUAGE] of the publication entitled [NAME OF THE BOOK] (hereinafter referred to as "the Work") and to market its translation rights in [COUNTRY OF THE TRANSLATOR] in order to find a local publisher to buy those rights and publish the [LANGUAGE] edition;

NOW THEREFORE, in consideration of the mutual promises hereinafter set forth, the Publisher and the Translator-Agent agree as follows:

1. TRANSLATION

1.1 The Translator-Agent shall do the translation of the Work into [LANGUAGE], including editing, proofreading, and final correction, according to the Publisher's guidelines. The deadline for delivery of the translation of the Work is [DATE OF DELIVERY]. Any modification of this deadline after the Effective Date at the Translator-Agent's request will take effect only if both parties agree to such modification, and said modification of the date of delivery shall be expressed in writing as an additional act of this contract. If the Translator-Agent does not meet the second agreed deadline for delivery, the Publisher has the right to terminate the Contract with no compensation due for the partial translation work of the Translator-Agent.

1.2 The translation shall be made faithfully and accurately, shall be of high literary quality, and shall consist of the whole of the textual, pictorial, diagrammatic material, and software constituting the Work. The Translator-Agent shall do the translation without alteration, additions, or deletions, except with the permission of the Publisher or at his request. The Publisher has the right to suggest corrections to the translation. The Publisher reserves the right to approve the final translation manuscript before its publication.

1.3 The manuscript of the Work will be provided by the Publisher in an appropriate editable format agreed upon by both parties. During the translation work, the Publisher shall offer continuous support to the translator, answering any questions the Translator-Agent has about the text. The Publisher must inform the Translator-Agent about any specific language difficulties, semantics and shades of meaning he may encounter, and any necessity of changing some wording to conform to the foreign language of the translation, and to differences in culture and place, if any.

1.4 The translation work of the Translator-Agent is evaluated at [AMOUNT] [CURRENCY] per [NUMBER IN WORDS]

(*[NUMBER IN FIGURES]*) words of the *source document / translated document*.
If the Translator-Agent's marketing campaign is successful, as defined in Paragraph 2.5 of this Contract, the above sum is payable by the Publisher entirely, as the due translation fee. The entire due translation fee shall be paid by the Publisher to the Translator-Agent within *[NUMBER IN WORDS]* (*[NUMBER IN FIGURES]*) days from the date the Publisher receives his own translation fee from the buying publisher.
If the Translator-Agent marketing campaign is unsuccessful and no buyer is found for the translation rights, the Translator-Agent shall be paid only the guarantees set forth in Article 3 of this Contract, within the time frames specified in the same article.

2. FOREIGN REPRESENTATION

2.1 The Translator-Agent shall run a marketing campaign targeting local publishers in his country of residence in order to find a buyer for the translation rights for the Work. The marketing campaign shall consist of contacting publishers and presenting the offer for licensing the translation rights for the Work.
The Translator-Agent represents the Publisher in his country of residence and acts in Publisher's behalf with respect only to the current campaign of licensing the translation rights of the Work.

2.2 The marketing campaign shall start after the date of delivery of the translation and after the Publisher puts the translated Work in the final form, and shall end when the Translator-Agent finds a buyer for the translation rights license in that country, with said buyer signing a contract of licensing the translation rights with the Publisher. The marketing campaign shall be conducted under the Publisher's guidelines and training provided to the Translator-Agent, but under Translator-Agent's own management regarding sheduling, daily amount of work, and methods of contact.

2.3 The time interval for the Translator-Agent to find a buyer for the translation rights of the Work in his country is [NUMBER IN WORDS] ([NUMBER IN FIGURES]) days after the Publisher puts the delivered translation in its final form and forwards it to the Translator-Agent. Any modification of this deadline after the Effective Date at the Translator-Agent's request will take effect effect only if both parties agree to such modification, and said modification of the specified time interval shall be expressed in writing as an additional act of this contract.
The deadline for finding a buyer is considered as met if a local publisher declares his intention to buy the translation rights of the Work and establishes contact with the Publisher regarding this transaction, either before or on the date of the deadline.

2.4 If a potential buyer who declared his intention to buy the translation rights before the deadline fails to sign a written agreement with the Publisher for this sale, for any reason, the Publisher must inform the Translator-Agent of the failure to reach agreement, whereupon the Translator-Agent may resume and continue the marketing campaign until the deadline for finding another buyer. If the Publisher informs the Translator-Agent after the established deadline of the failure to reach agreement, the Translator-Agent and the Publisher should agree on an extension of this deadline, this agreement being expressed in writing as an additional act to this Contract.

2.5 The Translator-Agent's campaign is declared successful as to having found a buyer when the agreement of licensing the translation rights is signed by the two publishers involved. When such agreement is signed, the Translator-Agent is eligible to receive the agent commission from the Publisher, in the amount of [PERCENTAGE IN NUMERALS]% of the list price of the new edition, in [CURRENCY], which includes any advance against royalties and regular royalties earned by the Publisher from the local buying publisher.

The agent commission shall be paid by the Publisher to the Translator-Agent each time the Publisher receives a payment from the local buying publisher, no later than [*NUMBER IN WORDS*] ([*NUMBER IN FIGURES*]) days from that payment. After that interval, delays in due agent commission payments are subject to penalties for the Publisher of [*PERCENTAGE IN NUMERALS*]% of the due amount per delayed day.

2.6 The agent commission is not due by the Publisher to the Translator-Agent if the local publisher who bought the license for the translation of the Work delays or misses a payment. That agent commission shall be paid after the amount due is recovered from the local publisher.
The agent commissions remain in effect as long as the written agreement for licensing the translation rights of the Work is active. Any extension of this agreement after its termination, or a new agreement having as subject the same Work, generates the obligation of the Publisher to pay agent commissions to the Translator-Agent in the same percentage as agreed upon in this Contract and under the same terms.

2.7 After the agreement for licensing the translation rights of the Work is signed, the Translator-Agent shall maintain regular communication with the local publisher in his country regarding the normal flow of the collaboration between the two publishers, and should intervene through amicable discussions in the case of any eventual delayed due payments of royalties, in order to hasten the local publisher's payment of royalties to the Publisher.

3. GUARANTEES

3.1 As a minimum guarantee for the Translator-Agent's work in case of an unsuccessful marketing campaign (no licensing translation rights agreement signed), the Publisher shall pay to the Translator-Agent the following sums:

a) [*PERCENTAGE IN NUMERALS*]% of the due translation fee, as evaluated in Paragraph 1.4.
b) Royalties of [*PERCENTAGE IN NUMERALS*]% of the list price of a future [*LANGUAGE OF TRANSLATION*] edition published by the Publisher himself.
c) Other guarantees: [*DESCRIPTION*].
[If one of the above guarantee types is not offered, the respective option should be removed from the contract, as well as any further references to said guarantee in the next Paragraph.]
The guarantees shall be paid in [*CURRENCY*].

3.2 The guarantee described in part a) in Paragraph 3.1 is payable by the Publisher after the deadline for finding a buyer, but no later than [*NUMBER IN WORDS*] ([*NUMBER IN FIGURES*]) days from that deadline.
The guarantee described in part b) in Paragraph 3.1 is payable by the Publisher after the publication of the new edition, with [*MONTHLY/QUARTERLY/SEMESTERLY/YEARLY*] frequency, in [*NUMBER IN WORDS*] ([*NUMBER IN FIGURES*]) days from the end of the regular period, if sales occurred during that period. The Publisher shall, prior to payment, send a detailed report of the number of copies sold during that period.
[If guarantees of type a) are not offered and thus not mentioned in Paragraph 3.1, the following Paragraph 3.3 shall be inserted in the current Article:]

3.3 The Publisher commits to publish the translation of the Work provided by the Translator-Agent as a new edition of the Work and put it on his distribution channels in a period of [*NUMBER IN WORDS*] ([*NUMBER IN FIGURES*]) days from the deadline of finding a buyer as stated in Paragraph 2.3.
If the Publisher does not publish this new edition within the aforementioned period, he is liable for paying to the Translator-Agent the full translation fee as evaluated in Paragraph 1.4. That sum is due from the first day after that period and is subject to

penalties for the Publisher of [*PERCENTAGE IN NUMERALS*]% of the due amount per delayed day.

4. GRANT & COPYRIGHT

4.1 The Translator-Agent hereby grants and assigns to the Publisher the right to print, publish, reproduce, distribute, license, and sell the translation of the Work in [*LANGUAGE*], including the exclusive right to sell or to license others to sell said translation in volume form throughout the World. The copyright terms stated in this Article refer to all possible versions of the translation of the Work with respect to support (paper, electronic storage devices, or film/microfilm) and type (classical book, electronic book, or audio book).

4.2 If the Publisher pays to the Translator-Agent any fee for the translation work, either the entire translation fee as evaluated in Paragraph 1.4 if the license is sold *or a partial translation fee as guarantee, as stated in Paragraph 3.1, if the license is not sold as result of Translator-Agent's marketing campaign*, the copyright of the translation is owned entirely by the Publisher. This ownership comes into effect in the moment of payment of the translation fee. [*The previous portion in italics should be removed if guarantees of type a) are not offered.*]

4.3 If the Publisher does not pay to the Translator-Agent any fee for the translation work, neither partial nor full, as agreed according to this Contract and as the result of Translator-Agent's unsuccessful marketing campaign, the copyright of the translation of the Work shall be shared by both parties of this Contract and neither party can publish, license, or distribute the translation of the Work by any means, freely or not, without the written approval of the other or a written agreement having as its subject the common ownership of its copyright.

If at any time after the termination of this Contract the Publisher pays to the Translator-Agent a translation fee agreed by both parties at one party's proposal, the copyright of the translation of the Work shall revert entirely to the Publisher.

4.4 In all situations, the Translator-Agent keeps the intellectual rights to the translation of the Work. Any further publication of the translation of the Work by the Publisher shall mention on the copyright page of the new edition the name of the Translator-Agent as translator of the original Work. The Publisher shall not alter the content of the published translation of the Work in any way, through additions, deletions, or changes, except with the written approval of the Translator-Agent.
If the Contract is terminated due to failure of the Translator-Agent to meet the deadline for delivery of the translation, according to Paragraph 5.3, the Publisher may not use any partial translation delivered by the Translator-Agent for completing the translation through another translator or for publishing separately, except with the written approval of the Translator-Agent. In case the partial translation is used, the name of the Translator-Agent shall be included along with the new translator's name on the copyright page of the published edition, unless both parties agree not to mention the Translator-Agent's name.

4.5 All the data collected by the Translator-Agent during his own marketing campaign (local publishers' contact data, specific information regarding their activity, the history of contacts and replies, and the entire database created) remain his property and he may use it at any time for other purposes not related to this Contract, both during this Contract and after its termination.

4.6 In all situations, the Translator-Agent shall keep the electronic manuscript of the translation of the Work only on his personal computer and/or his personal data storage devices. The Translator-Agent does not have the right to transmit the electronic manuscript to third parties, except with the approval of the Publisher, during this Contract or after it terminates, as described in Article 5.

5. TERMINATION OF THIS CONTRACT

5.1 This Contract shall be rendered invalid if not signed by the Translator-Agent within [*NUMBER IN WORDS*] ([*NUMBER IN FIGURES*]) days of the Effective Date.

5.2 This Contract shall terminate at any time if both parties agree on its termination. Such termination may be subject to negotiation regarding any due sums set forth in Article 1, Article 2, and Article 3, which otherwise remain payable under the conditions described in respective articles.

5.3 This Contract shall terminate if the Translator-Agent does not meet the deadline for delivery of the translation of the Work, unless the two parties agree prior to deadline to an extension of the delivery date and shall terminate if the second agreed deadline is not met. In this latter case, no sum is due to the Translator-Agent.

5.4 This Contract shall terminate if the Translator-Agent does not meet the deadline for finding a buyer for the translation rights of the Work, unless the two parties agree prior to deadline to an extension of this deadline and shall terminate if the second agreed deadline is not met. In this latter case, the Publisher owes to the Translator-Agent the offered guarantees described in Article 3.

5.5 Upon termination of this Contract:
No party shall be liable for any termination damages or indemnities, and the Translator-Agent agrees not to restrain the Publisher from appointing an alternate collaboration or from

acting directly with respect to the licensing of existing and future translation rights in [COUNTRY OF THE TRANSLATOR].
All the copyrights of this Work shall revert to the Publisher, except in the case described in Paragraph 5.4, in which case no translation fee is paid to the Translator-Agent as guarantee. In this event, the copyright of the translation of the Work shall be shared by both parties, as defined in Paragraph 4.3.

6. LEGAL JURISDICTION

This Contract shall be construed and interpreted under and in accordance with the laws of [COUNTRY OF THE PUBLISHER]. The parties irrevocably (a) agree that any suit, action, or other legal proceeding arising out of this Contract may be brought in any court located in [COUNTRY OF THE PUBLISHER], and (b) consent to the Jurisdiction of any such court in any suit, action, or proceeding.

7. GIVING NOTICE

All notices, requests, and demands (e.g., address changes, termination requests, various copies of receipts, etc.) given to or made upon these parties shall be in writing and shall be properly addressed, postage prepaid, sent via registered or certified mail, or personally delivered to such party. Notices may be sent by facsimile transmission provided that, in addition, a copy of such facsimile shall be sent by mail to each addressee. The effective date of a notice for purposes of this Contract shall be the date on which such notice was actually received by the party to whom it is addressed. Each party shall promptly notify the other party of any address change.

To the Publisher at:
[ADDRESS, PHONE, FAX, AND CONTACT PERSON OF THE PUBLISHER]
To the Translator-Agent at:
[ADDRESS, PHONE, FAX OF THE TRANSLATOR-AGENT]

8. ENTIRETY OF CONTRACT

This Contract, together with any exhibits hereto, constitutes the sole and entire agreement between the parties pertaining to the subject matter hereof and supersedes all prior negotiations, dealings, letters of intent, agreements, and understandings of the parties in connection therewith. No amendment, modification, or alteration of this Contract shall be valid unless it shall be in writing and signed by the parties hereto.

9. HEADINGS

THE HEADINGS of this Contract are included for convenience only and are not part of this Contract.

IN WITNESS WHEREOF duplicate copies of this Contract have been signed on behalf of the Publisher by its duly authorized officer, and by the Translator-Agent, on the dates specified below.

[*NAME OF THE PUBLISHER*]

By: (*SIGNATURE*)

Name: [*NAME OF THE PUBLISHER'S DULY AUTHORIZED OFFICER*]
Title: [*TITLE OF THE PUBLISHER'S DULY AUTHORIZED OFFICER*]
Date: [*SIGNING DATE*]

[*NAME OF THE TRANSLATOR-AGENT*]

By: (*SIGNATURE*)

Name: [*NAME OF THE TRANSLATOR-AGENT*]
Date: [*SIGNING DATE*]

Appendix 3 – *Translation Rights Contract*

TRANSLATION RIGHTS CONTRACT

CONTRACT made this [DATE] (hereinafter referred to as "Effective Date") by and between [SELLING PUBLISHER'S NAME] of [SELLING PUBLISHER'S ADDRESS] (hereinafter referred to as the "Original Publisher"], and [BUYING PUBLISHER'S NAME] of [COUNTRY OF THE BUYING PUBLISHER] (hereinafter referred to as the "Foreign Publisher"), with his principal mailing address as [MAILING ADDRESS OF FOREIGN PUBLISHER]:

WHEREAS the Original Publisher is the sole and exclusive owner of the rights which are the subject of this contract; and

WHEREAS the Foreign Publisher desires to obtain the rights to publish the [LANGUAGE] edition, (hereinafter referred to as "Translation" of the publication entitled [NAME OF THE BOOK] (hereinafter referred to as "the Work");

NOW THEREFORE, in consideration of the mutual promises hereinafter set forth, the Oelling Publisher and the Foreign Publisher agree as follows:

1. GRANT & TERRITORY
The Original Publisher hereby grants and assigns to the Foreign Publisher the right to print, publish, reproduce, distribute, license, and sell the [EDITION NUMBER] edition in [LANGUAGE] of the Work, including the exclusive right to sell or to license others to sell said translation in volume form only throughout the

following:
[TERRITORY/TERRITORIES/COUNTRY/COUNTRIES]
This Contract does not grant any rights with respect to subsequent editions of the Work.

2. ROYALTY RATES ON SALES AND REMAINDERS

With respect to all copies of the Translation sold, the Foreign Publisher shall pay to the Original Publisher in [CURRENCY], royalties as follows, based on the local list price received by the Foreign Publisher for sales of the Translation: [PERCENTAGE IN NUMERALS]%. The Foreign Publisher shall sell no copies of the Work as remainders within a period of [NUMBER IN WORDS] ([NUMBER IN FIGURES]) years after the first publication. If after this [NUMBER IN WORDS]-year period, the Foreign Publisher wishes to dispose of any surplus stock as remainders at a reduced price, the Foreign Publisher shall first notify the Original Publisher of his intention. Royalty to be paid to the Original Publisher on all copies sold as remainders shall be [PERCENTAGE IN WORDS] percent ([PERCENTAGE IN FIGURES]%) of the sum received by the Foreign Publisher; however, no royalty shall be payable to the Original Publisher on remainders sold at or below the Foreign Publisher's cost of paper, printing, and binding.

3. MINIMUM GUARANTEE

As a minimum guarantee of royalty, the Foreign Publisher shall pay to the Original Publisher within [NUMBER IN WORDS] ([NUMBER IN FIGURES]) days of signing this Contract the nonrefundable sum of [AMOUNT] [CURRENCY]. Said sum shall be considered as an advance against royalties that may become due hereunder; however, in the event accrued royalties total less than this amount, the Original Publisher shall retain the full amount paid pursuant to this Paragraph.

The Foreign Publisher shall pay the cost of all taxes and preparatory fees necessary to pay the minimum guarantee.

4. REPORTS AND ROYALTY PAYMENTS

With respect to reporting on copies published and sold and paying of royalties, the Foreign Publisher shall:

a. Immediately upon publication of the Translation, submit to the Original Publisher by fax or airmail a statement giving (1) the date of publication, (2) the total number of copies printed, and (3) the retail price, said statement to be accompanied by four (4) copies of the initial printing.

b. Within [NUMBER IN WORDS] ([NUMBER IN FIGURES]) days after January 1 and July 1, submit to the Original Publisher a statement concerning such preceding six (6) months giving (1) the date and current retail price of any reprint of the Work, (2) the total number of copies printed by the Foreign Publisher, if any, (3) the total number of copies sold by or on behalf of the Foreign Publisher, and (4) the number of copies remaining on hand at the end of the reporting period, said statement to be accompanied by the corresponding royalty payment required under Paragraph 2 of the Contract.

c. The Foreign Publisher shall permit his books of account or records of sale to be inspected at any reasonable time during normal business hours by a representative of the Original Publisher for the purpose of verifying the amounts due hereunder.

d. In the event of termination of this Contract, the Foreign Publisher shall within [NUMBER IN WORDS] ([NUMBER IN FIGURES]) days submit (1) a final report which provides the data required in 4.b, and (2) detailed documentation of any royalties owed.

e. The exchange rate to be used in computing the sums owed by the Foreign Publisher to the Original Publisher in [CURRENCY] shall be the exchange rate in effect on the appropriate day of the Reporting Period (December 31 or June 30) as reported in the [TITLE OF A FINANCIAL PUBLICATION].

f. Any local taxes levied or passed on to the Original Publisher for the royalty payments shall be borne by the Foreign Publisher.

5. FAITHFUL TRANSLATION

The Original Publisher shall provide the Foreign Publisher with the translation of the Work done by the Original Publisher's own translators. The Original Publisher agrees to obtain from all his translators proper written grants of all rights to their work. The translation shall be made faithfully and accurately, shall be of good literary quality, and shall consist of the whole of the textual, pictorial, diagrammatic material, and software constituting the Work. The translation manuscript will be provided by the Original Publisher in a proper editable format agreed upon by both publishers. The Foreign Publisher shall publish the Translation without alteration, abridgment, or supplement, except with the express written permission of the Original Publisher. The Original Publisher reserves the right to approve the final manuscript before its publication. The Foreign Publisher will submit the final manuscript to the Original Publisher for review. Any comments will be forwarded to the Foreign Publisher and required modifications made to the manuscript before the Translation is published. The Original Publisher shall forward modifications of the manuscript within a reasonable time period. The Foreign Publisher agrees to use the original cover art and design of the Work. The Foreign Publisher must obtain written approval from the Original Publisher of the final cover of the Translation before its publication.

6. COST OF TRANSLATION AND PERMISSIONS

All costs and expenses of carrying out the Foreign Publisher's rights and performing the Foreign Publisher's obligations hereunder shall be borne by the Foreign Publisher, including the costs of compensating the translation work. The Foreign Publisher shall pay to the Original Publisher upon signing this Contract the nonrefundable sum of [*AMOUNT*] [*CURRENCY*] as the fee for the provided translation work. The Foreign Publisher must pay to the Original Publisher this advance within [*NUMBER IN WORDS*] ([*NUMBER IN FIGURES*]) days of signing this Contract. The Foreign Publisher shall also be responsible for obtaining and paying for any permissions for the use of photographs, illustrations, or quotations from works copyrighted by any person or persons or entities other than the Original Publisher, which are required in connection with the Translation.

7. SALES PROMOTION

The Foreign Publisher shall exert every reasonable effort to promote the sale of the Translation licensed hereunder.

8. GOING OUT OF PRINT

The Foreign Publisher shall provide the Original Publisher with written notice of his intention to permit the Translation to go out of print. For purposes of this Contract, the Translation may be considered out of print if the Foreign Publisher or another agency on behalf of the Foreign Publisher sells fewer than two hundred fifty (250) copies in two successive six-month periods.

9. DURATION AND TERMINATION OF THIS CONTRACT

a. This Contract shall be rendered invalid if not signed by the Foreign Publisher within [*NUMBER IN WORDS*] ([*NUMBER IN FIGURES*]) days of the Effective Date.

b. This Contract shall terminate if the sum due upon signing under Paragraph 3 above has not been received by the Original Publisher within the time specified in Paragraph 3.

c. This Contract shall terminate [*NUMBER IN WORDS*] ([*NUMBER IN FIGURES*]) months after the release of any subsequent editions of the Work, unless otherwise agreed in writing.

d. The Foreign Publisher agrees to publish the Translation within [*NUMBER IN WORDS*] ([*NUMBER IN FIGURES*]) months of the Effective Date. If the Foreign Publisher fails to publish the Translation within the specified time, unless the Original Publisher grants a written extension, this Contract shall terminate.

e. If the Foreign Publisher allows the Translation to go out of print for more than [*NUMBER IN WORDS*] ([*NUMBER IN FIGURES*]) months, all rights to the Translation under this Contract will revert to the Original Publisher.

f. At the election of the Original Publisher if the Foreign Publisher shall fail, within [*NUMBER IN WORDS*] ([*NUMBER IN FIGURES*]) days after notice is given by the Original Publisher that the latter is in default with respect to any of the terms of this Contract, to remedy such default to the satisfaction of the Original Publisher, then the Original Publisher may terminate this Contract.

g. The Original Publisher shall have the right to terminate this Contract if ownership or control of the Foreign Publisher is changed.

Upon termination of this Contract:

h. The Original Publisher shall not be liable for any termination damages or indemnities, and the Foreign Publisher hereby agrees not to restrain the Original Publisher from appointing an alternate licensee or from acting directly in respect of existing and future translations.

i. If there is remaining stock, the Foreign Publisher agrees to sell such stock within [*NUMBER IN WORDS*] ([*NUMBER IN FIGURES*]) days, unless otherwise agreed in writing.

j. All the rights hereunder shall revert to the Original Publisher, without prejudice to any monies due the Original Publisher from the Foreign Publisher.

10. COPYRIGHT OWNERSHIP, PROTECTION, AND NOTICES

The Foreign Publisher shall, upon the publication of the Translation, promptly secure whatever copyright protection may be available in the aforesaid territory with respect to the Translation. All copyrights in the Work shall be and shall remain owned by the Original Publisher, subject only to the rights granted to the Foreign Publisher herein. The Foreign Publisher shall display in [*ORIGINAL LANGUAGE OF THE WORK*], in all copies of the Translation in the place which is customary in the publishing practice of his country, the original title of the Work and the name(s) and affiliation(s) as shown on the title page of the Translation in this form:

© [*NAME OF THE FOREIGN PUBLISHER*] [*YEAR OF FIRST PUBLICATION OF THE TRANSLATION*]. Authorized translation of the [*ORIGINAL LANGUAGE OF THE WORK*] edition © [*YEAR OF FIRST PUBLICATION OF THE ORIGINAL EDITION*] [*NAME OF THE ORIGINAL PUBLISHER*]. This translation is published and sold by permission of [*NAME OF THE ORIGINAL PUBLISHER*], who is the owner of all rights to publish and sell the same.

The Foreign Publisher shall also include any other notice required by the applicable copyright laws for the full protection of the Work or the Translation. The provisions of this Paragraph are of the essence of this Contract, and the permission to publish and sell the Translation which is granted hereby is conditioned upon the printing of the aforesaid copyright notices on each copy thereof. Ownership of the copyright of the Translation shall not entitle the Foreign Publisher to make or permit any use of the Translation other than as permitted by Paragraph 1 hereof, and the Foreign Publisher's only rights in and to the Work or the Translation are those granted by Paragraph 1.

11. INFRINGEMENT OF COPYRIGHTS

In the event the copyright in the Foreign Publisher's edition shall be infringed within the territory of the grant, the Foreign Publisher shall take such steps as may be necessary to restrain such infringement, and in the event that the Foreign Publisher shall collect damages therefore, then the Foreign Publisher shall thereupon pay to the Original Publisher one-half of all sums so collected after deduction of legal expenses and court fees paid by the Foreign Publisher in enjoining said infringement and effecting the collection of said sums. The Original Publisher shall have the right and option to engage counsel of his own choosing, to join with the Foreign Publisher in any action to restrain infringement, or to bring an action separately in the name of the Original Publisher or Licensee.

12. ASSIGNMENT OF LICENSE

The Foreign Publisher shall not assign this license nor shall the Foreign Publisher sublicense its rights without the prior written consent of the Original Publisher.

13. RESERVATION OF RIGHTS

All rights not specifically granted to the Foreign Publisher in this Contract are reserved by the Original Publisher.

14. WARRANTIES AND COVENANTS

The Foreign Publisher represents, warrants, and covenants that he has full power to enter into this Contract and to perform the services required hereunder; that any advertising or promotional statements which he publishes concerning the Translation will not, in whole or in part, plagiarize any work, infringe any copyright, or violate any right of privacy or other personal or property right, or contain false, misleading, fraudulent, libelous, or obscene matter or other matter which is unlawful or which will give rise to a criminal or civil cause of action; and that he shall at all times in the conduct of the promotion, distribution, and sale of the Translation strictly comply with all applicable laws and regulations of the Territory. The Foreign Publisher shall indemnify and hold the Original Publisher, his officers, directors, employees or agents harmless from any loss, expense (including reasonable attorney's fees and disbursements) or damages incurred by the Foreign Publisher or any of his officers, directors, employees, or agents as a result of a breach of any of the foregoing warranties and covenants, or any such loss, expense or damage arising from any claim, demand, recovery, suit motion, or civil or criminal proceeding based upon or alleging in any way, in whole or in part, facts which are contrary to, or inconsistent with, any of the foregoing warranties and covenants. These warranties and indemnities shall survive the termination of this Contract.

15. [COUNTRY OF THE SELLING PUBLISHER] EXPORT CONTROLS

The Original Publisher's books and other technical data are of [COUNTRY OF SELLING PUBLISHER] origin and, as such, are subject to export licensing and other restrictions under [COUNTRY OF SELLING PUBLISHER] law. The Original Publisher will provide information regarding [COUNTRY OF SELLING PUBLISHER] government export and re-export requirements upon request. The Foreign Publisher shall comply with all applicable restrictions on exports and re-exports, including obtaining any required [COUNTRY OF SELLING PUBLISHER] or local government license, authorization, or approval. Whenever the Foreign Publisher re-sells or otherwise disposes of any the Original Publisher's products or other technical data, it will inform each transferee of all applicable requirements and restrictions of further exports or re-exports. The Foreign Publisher will furnish the Original Publisher such documents and information with respect to export control in such form as the Original Publisher may from time to time require.

16. LEGAL JURISDICTION

This Contract shall be construed and interpreted under and in accordance with the laws of [COUNTRY OF SELLING PUBLISHER]. The parties irrevocably (a) agree that any suit, action or other legal proceeding arising out of this Contract may be brought in any court located in [COUNTRY OF SELLING

PUBLISHER], and (b) consent to the Jurisdiction of any such court in any suit, action, or proceeding.

17. GIVING NOTICE
All notices, requests, and demands (e.g., address changes, termination requests, various copies of receipts, etc.) given to or made upon the parties shall be in writing and shall be properly addressed, postage prepaid, sent via registered or certified mail, or personally delivered to such party. Notices may be sent by facsimile transmission provided that, in addition, a copy of such facsimile shall be sent by mail to each addressee. The effective date of a notice for purposes of this Contract shall be the date on which such notice was actually received by the party to whom it is addressed. Each party shall promptly notify the other party of any address change.
To the Original Publisher at:
[*ADDRESS, PHONE, FAX, AND CONTACT PERSON OF SELLING PUBLISHER*]
To the Foreign Publisher at:
[*ADDRESS, PHONE, FAX, AND CONTACT PERSON OF BUYING PUBLISHER*]

18. ENTIRETY OF CONTRACT
This Contract, together with any exhibits hereto, constitutes the sole and entire agreement between the parties pertaining to the subject matter hereof and supersedes all prior negotiations, dealings, letters of intent, agreements, and understandings of the parties in connection therewith. No amendment, modification, or alteration of this Contract shall be valid unless it shall be in writing and signed by the parties hereto.

19. HEADINGS
THE HEADINGS of this Contract are included for convenience only and are not part of this Contract.

IN WITNESS WHEREOF duplicate copies of this Contract have been signed on behalf of the Original Publisher by his duly authorized officer, and on behalf of the Foreign Publisher by his duly authorized officer, on the dates specified below.

[NAME OF THE SELLING PUBLISHER]	**[NAME OF THE BUYING PUBLISHER]**
By: (*SIGNATURE*)	By: (*SIGNATURE*)
Name: [*NAME OF SELLING PUBLISHER'S DULY AUTHORIZED OFFICER*] Title: [*TITLE OF SELLING PUBLISHER'S DULY AUTHORIZED OFFICER*] Date: [*SIGNING DATE*]	Name: [*NAME OF BUYING PUBLISHER'S DULY AUTHORIZED OFFICER*] Title: [*TITLE OF BUYING PUBLISHER'S DULY AUTHORIZED OFFICER*] Date: [*SIGNING DATE*]

www.ingramcontent.com/pod-product-compliance
Lightning Source LLC
Chambersburg PA
CBHW072201160426
43197CB00012B/2483